MW01707467

Beyond the Blue Line

Volume 2

Sixty-Four New Stories
From the Other Side of Law Enforcement

To Barbara
Hope you enjoy the stories!
Thanks—

Joe D. Guy

3/07

PublishAmerica
Baltimore

© 2005 by Joe D. Guy.
All rights reserved. No part of this book may be reproduced, stored in a retrieval system or transmitted in any form or by any means without the prior written permission of the publishers, except by a reviewer who may quote brief passages in a review to be printed in a newspaper, magazine or journal.

First printing

ISBN: 1-4137-8202-7
PUBLISHED BY PUBLISHAMERICA, LLLP
www.publishamerica.com
Baltimore

Printed in the United States of America

Dedications

This book is dedicated to the memories of some good cops who have passed away since the publication of BBL Volume 1. They were more than just good cops; they also happened to be my friends.

Sgt. Gary "Bugs" Smith
Etowah Police Department, Polk County Sheriff's Department, Englewood Police Department

Chief Hershel Jack
Athens Police Department, Englewood Police Department, McMinn County Sheriff's Department

Officer Ronnie Bohannon
Etowah Police Department, McMinn County Sheriff's Department, Englewood Police Department, Athens Police Department

And to the memory of my first EMS partner, who showed me more than just the ropes, but rather how to find ways to laugh when I saw things that made me want to cry:
Paramedic Tony Coe

Blessed are the peacemakers
Who've walked upon these grounds,
In the faces on these walls
Their pride and courage still are found.
So when you pass this way, recall
Fallen comrades brave and bold,
And find yourself a worthy heart
To wear their badge of gold.

Tennessee Law Enforcement Training Academy
Class 718
J.Guy, McMinn County Sheriff's Department
1994

Acknowledgments

This collection of sixty-four articles from my syndicated newspaper column, "Beyond the Blue Line," would not have been possible were it not for the following friends and fellow cops, deputies, investigators, troopers, EMTs, paramedics, fire and rescue personnel, dispatchers, attorneys, and other emergency workers:

Law Enforcement and Criminal Justice: Matt Blair, Clinton "Pumpy" Tudors, Marc Threet, Ron McDonald, David McVey, Greg Obie, Sheriff Steve Frisbie, Kenny Coleman, Lt. Bill Farmer, Chris Baker, Becky Eaton, Terry Wilson, Brad Lane, Penny Alexander Richardello, Fred Schultz, Chief Tim Smith, Randy Ayers, Terry Elliott, Richard Brogan, Chief Danny McDonald, Steve Moore, Herb Adams, George Jorgenson, Danny Jones, Scott Ervin, David Guy, Paul St. John Fleming, Bill Matthews, Rick Cornett

Fire and Emergency Medical Services: Bruce and Darnita Collins, Mike Frost, Tim Evans, Ken Fryar, Johnny Lipps, Bill Roach, Lance McConkey, Jim Bruce Haney, Dr. Don Hardison, and many, many others.

Special thanks to the following editors of other publications who've carried my work: Doug Headrick, Ingrid Bueller, Arnold Ajello, and Toby Pendergrass.

To my boss, McMinn County, TN, Mayor John M. Gentry, for the opportunity he has given me and for his continued support, I am eternally indebted to him.

Finally, to my wife whose critical eye gave much needed editing and advice toward taste and censorship.

And to my three boys, who all think daddy tells a pretty good story.

Introduction

A lot of writers get asked the question: *How did you start writing?* I suppose that many give a soul-searching answer about how they felt they had to write in order to release some inner story or some other deep emotional need that needed to be fulfilled. When I get asked the same question, my response is a bit different.

You see, I began writing because I have a terrible memory.

During my career as a police officer and deputy sheriff, I was often present when a group of officers gathered to gossip and tell stories (usually on the night shift) in some out of the way eating establishment (a convenience store with a deli) and drink diet drinks and eat healthy foods (black coffee and donuts).

It was at these gatherings that we talked about different calls we'd responded to, people we'd met, things we'd done, times we'd been angry or terrified, and other stories where something simply humorous had happened. After an hour or so of passing tales around, we'd go back out to our patrol cars and resume working. For us, it was a time to release some stress and to share our experiences. But we never talked about those things with anyone else because none of us ever thought anyone outside of law enforcement or emergency services would want to hear about them.

But like I said, I have a terrible memory.

In order to keep a record of things that happened to me or things that were told to me by other cops, I started writing the stories down. The funny ones were what I began with, but over time I began recording the bad things, the terrible things that I saw or that other officers saw. I found that by writing those sad things down, I was able to deal with the situations a little better. I was able to find some closure, rather than carry those things around in my mind.

I had collected quite a few when I remembered something from my days at the state police academy. One of my instructors there, Sgt. Randy Tedford of the Oak Ridge, TN Police Department, had told us how he wrote a newspaper column about police work. I was, and continue to be, a big fan of David Hunter, an accomplished author and newspaper columnist with the *Knoxville News-Sentinel*, who writes from the perspective of an ex-cop. So I figured, *what the heck*.

I called my local newspaper and asked if they were looking for any new columnists. The editor, in a tone implying he'd heard this same song and dance before, said, "Not really, but you can send me what you've got." A week later a newspaper photographer showed up to take my picture and to inform me I was their newest columnist.

Now, several hundred articles, two books, and a novel later, I still find it hard to believe people actually do enjoy reading this stuff.

These stories are proof that "the truth is stranger than fiction." All are based on my own experiences or the experiences of fellow police officers, detectives, EMTs, paramedics, firefighters, rescue personnel, and dispatchers. While each story is true, I have sometimes taken the liberty to make certain changes to hide the specific locations and identities of the people involved.

But what you will read will hopefully give you a new perspective on the real world of law enforcement and emergency services. If nothing else, I hope to leave you with a deeper understanding of what these people do. Because to me they aren't just people, they are true heroes in uniform.

Contents

Part One

Most police officers, deputies, firefighters, EMTs, dispatchers, and rescue personnel will tell you that it's the funny things that help them get through their often stressful shifts. It's a phenomenon called "dark humor," and although it sometimes pokes fun at certain situations and people, it's more of a defense mechanism to keep emergency personnel from going crazy.

Ten Little, Nine Little, Eight Little Drunks

After receiving numerous complaints of drunk drivers in the area of a local bar, sheriff's deputies and highway patrol officers set up a roadblock nearby. Several intoxicated drivers were stopped in a matter of minutes as the bar closed, and its patrons attempted to swerve their way home.

Officers noticed one car driving particularly erratically, and of course, stopped the vehicle to investigate. Although it was a subcompact car, it was evident that several people were inside. The curiosity of the officers increased dramatically due to the strong smell of freshly smoked marijuana coming from inside the car. But no one inside seemed to have any knowledge of any such drug.

"How many have you got in there?" one of the State Troopers asked the driver.

"I dunno," came the reply.

"Looks like about six people," observed another officer, "I see two people in the front, and four in the back."

"Counting the driver?" asked the Trooper.

"Oh, yeah." Answered the deputy. "It must be seven."

One by one, each passenger was asked to exit out of the driver's door. Each was asked to perform a field sobriety test, and each was searched for possible narcotics. As the group of men standing behind the car increased, the officers were amazed at how many men were found to be in the car. And even more interesting was the fact that they were all tall and hefty men, at that, most standing at least several inches taller than the officers.

"I've got five guys out here," said the Trooper. "Is that car about empty yet?"

"Still several people in here," said the deputy, shining his flashlight on the faces inside. Still more big men were removed from the tiny car and were questioned and searched. All were in various stages of drunkenness, but all seemed very cooperative with the officers. Still, no marijuana had been found.

At last, the officer shined his light into the back seat, and announced, "Finally! We've only got two left in here! How many will that make?"

The Trooper took a quick head count of the men standing on the side of the road. "That'll make nine." He watched as the two men got out and walked toward him. But as they were searched, the officer at the car called for the Trooper to come up.

"You need to see this," said the officer, pointing his light into the back seat. The Trooper looked with disbelief at the form of a small-built man who sat squeezed down into the seat. He had been riding underneath all the other men.

"Make that ten," said the Trooper, motioning for the man to get out.

"We ain't doin' nuthin'," Complained the short man, who seemed not to share the cooperative attitude of his fellow passengers. "We was just goin' home. We had a designated driver."

The trooper pointed to the drunk driver in the back seat of his patrol car. "You mean that guy? Look, pal, having a designated driver only counts if he's sober." It was at that point that the Trooper saw the bag of marijuana lying beside the car at the man's feet.

"Is that yours?"

"Is what mine?" sneered the man.

"The *dope* in front of you," said the Trooper.

The man simply spat on the ground near the Trooper's shiny shoes. "I bet you ain't so tough without that badge."

The deputy standing nearby rolled his eyes and said with a sigh, "Thank goodness it's the little guy who wants to fight."

But no such physical altercation was necessary. Since the big men knew that their short friend was the owner of the pot, they were very specific in their description of his future treatment if they were forced to go to jail on his behalf. The little man grumbled something under his breath, considering his options. It took him only a few minutes to reluctantly admit his guilt. After being handcuffed, the man was placed into the back of the Trooper's car with his friend.

"Look on the bright side," said the Trooper as he closed the door, "You'll be riding with your designated driver after all."

Angry Dispatchers, a Jig, and a Two-Step

The dispatcher took a sip of coffee and rubbed her tired eyes. It was almost 3:00 A.M., and once again the 911 line was ringing. She knew who she would find on the line before she snatched up the phone to answer it, and as she placed the phone to her ear, she immediately wished she had taken time to smoke a cigarette during her last break.

"911 Emergency."

For a few seconds, she heard nothing. Then an elderly man's voice mumbled something, then said, "Is this the police?"

"Yes, Mr. Billings," answered the dispatcher sharply, "this is the Emergency Communications Center. Just like it has been all night since you started calling hours ago." She glanced at the clock on her computer screen and then, with false pleasantry, said, "Can we help you?"

"Well," he began, "I's just calling to see…" His voice trailed off.

"To see what, Mr. Billings?"

"Well," he said again, "Just to see what you was doing…"

"Mr. Billings," said the agitated dispatcher, "You've got to stop calling this number unless you have an emergency."

"I do have an emergency," said the old man, "I can't sleep."

It's entirely too late for this, thought the angry dispatcher. But at the same time, she felt a hint of pity for the old man. For the past several years, he had been suffering from the early stages of Alzheimer's disease. As he became less and less lucid, he would call 911 late at night, sometimes several times a night, and just sit on the line mumbling incoherently. It was a cause of irritation to the emergency operators, as well as to the deputies who were repeatedly asked to go to the man's home to make sure he was all right and to ask him to stop calling the emergency lines.

Already, deputies had gone to Mr. Billings small house some four or five times this night, and again the dispatcher called over the radio to send another officer to speak with him.

"If there is anything you can do to get him to go to sleep and stop calling, we'd appreciate it," added the dispatcher.

"10-4," replied the officer. He hung up the radio mic and looked over at his female partner. The other officer leaned her head over on the cool window and stared out at the darkness.

"Everybody else has been out there tonight," she said, "so we might as well, too."

In a few minutes, the patrol car pulled up to the tiny, ill-kept residence of Mr. Billings. The small white house looked almost spooky with the dim light glowing through its tattered curtains. The officers left the car and walked up to the door. They knocked, and a thin, haggard old man dressed in dirty pants and a T-shirt opened the door.

"Good morning, Mr. Billings."

""What? Well, I guess so. You want to come in?" he said in a trembling voice.

The officers went inside the front room, one of only three rooms in the whole house. "Mr. Billings, have you been calling 911 again?" asked the male officer.

"I guess I have," sighed the old man wistfully, as he shuffled around the room. "I guess I have."

"Is everything alright?" questioned the female officer.

"Why, yes, I reckon so," mumbled the man.

"Well, we need you to stop calling 911, unless there is something wrong, Sir," said the male officer. Looking over the messy room.

"I just can't sleep...." complained Mr. Billings. But the officer had seen something in the darkened corner. Desperate for some way to resolve the situation, he began to think of a way to deal with what amounted to a tired and lonely old man.

"Say, Mr. Billings," said the deputy, "do you play that old guitar over there?"

The old man stopped his pacing and looked at the old guitar leaning in the corner. "I do sometimes."

"What kind of music do you like?"

"Oh, I like the old stuff," said Mr. Billings, as if he were suddenly alert. "You know, old bluegrass and such."

"I like that old stuff, too," said the officer, winking to his confused female partner. "And I play a little, too. I'll tell you what: If I play you some old tunes on that guitar, will you stop calling 911 tonight?"

The old man rubbed his unshaven chin. "Well, I 'spect that would be alright.... but now I'll stop gittin' on the phone if... well, if..."

"If what?" asked the deputy.

The old man pointed at the female officer and grinned sheepishly. "I'll stop callin' if she'll dance with me while you play some music."

The female officer took a step back. "Oh, no, now wait just a minute..."

"Oh, come on!" smiled her partner, reaching for the old guitar. "He promises he'll go to bed and stop calling if we do this, don't you Mr. Billings?"

"I shore do promise," he said with glee.

"Oh, brother," said the female deputy with a shake of her head. "This was never in my job description."

And so, as the moon shone over the little shack, the sounds of old bluegrass tunes were heard late into the night. And later, tired from dancing many a jig and two-step, the old man fell asleep, dreaming of friends and memories long faded and past.

"What's That On Top of My House?"

Now let me first say that I'm a believer. I have to be, I've got kids. But even if I didn't have these little voices to remind me that the Big Red Guy is about to make his yearly Christmas stop, I'd probably still believe in one way or another. Because, like most other police officers, I know that Santa Claus is real.

It could be that my knowledge of this fact was first confirmed about eleven years ago. While working the night shift on Christmas Eve, I heard another officer say over the radio that he had come upon a man walking. The officer told the dispatcher that he was going to transport the man to another location where a ride would pick him up. I happened to pass the other officer as he made his way across town. I almost ran out of the road when I saw a large man in the front seat beside him, dressed in red, with a white flowing beard. The passenger winked at me as he went by. I swear he did.

Strange things have always happened while working over the holiday that make me believe that something magical and jolly may be afoot. Christmas carols will suddenly and mysteriously play over the police radio. Red blinking lights are reported (and seen) in the midnight sky. Toys, clothing, and food appear out of nowhere for people in need. Candy, cookies, cakes, and other treats are found at the last place you would ever expect them to be, the jail. Very strange indeed.

I am told that the following exchange took place over the radio one Noel night:

"Control, this is Unit Twenty-One. Looks like I've come up on some livestock in the road. I'll be out trying to clear the highway."

"10-4," replied the sleepy dispatcher. A few minutes passed.

"Control, also be advised that I've located a vehicle in a ditch. Stand by to see if I'll need a wrecker."

"10-4."

A few more minutes passed.

"Control, this is Unit Twenty-One. I believe I've located the driver of the vehicle and owner of the animals. Can you check a driver's license for me?"

"Go ahead."

"Control, the first name is spelled K-R-I-S-S...."

"Go ahead with the last name," said the dispatcher as she typed the information into the computer system.

"Spelling of the last name is K-R-I-N-G-L-E."

The dispatcher typed along with the officer's voice, whispering a repeat of his transmission. "...I-N-G-L-E. Hey! Wait just a minute!"

"Control this is Unit Twenty-One." A slight giggle could be heard in the background. "Be advised that the vehicle was pulled out of the ditch by these strange-looking cows, and the owner has apparently flown from the scene. I'll be back on patrol."

And then there was the time an elderly lady called to report her house had been vandalized on Christmas morning. She was one of those poor old frightened souls who make several complaints a week about noises and strange cars in her neighborhood, and she was often tormented by young pranksters. The officers who responded found her angrily waiting in her front yard.

"They did it to me again!" she declared.

"Did what?" asked the officers.

"They threw that stuff up on my house."

The officers inspected the foul-smelling substance that was splattered over the roof and yard, and shook their heads in disgust.

"Yeah, that's cow manure, all right."

"Oh, no," said the woman with a stern look in her eye, "There ain't no cow that could get up there. That's from a reindeer."

The officers took their report, made notes of the evidence, and went on their way.

You can't argue with reason.

Drunks and SWAT Teams Equal a "Stone Cold" Mess

The SWAT team had assembled for their pre-mission briefing, and each officer listened closely as the narcotics detective drew the mission plan on an office blackboard. A drug-dealing operation had been found operating from a mobile home in a rural area, and today the SWAT team would be executing a high-risk search warrant on the premises. As was the norm, each officer had an individual job that would ensure the success not only of the mission, but more importantly the safety of the other officers and any suspects they would encounter. The level of stress rose with each passing moment, and each man prepared himself for any possible dangers that might lie ahead.

But delays are often a part of serving search warrants. Although the SWAT team was prepared to move, detectives had some difficulty in locating a judge to approve and sign the warrant in order for it to be served. While awaiting the return of the signed warrant, the tactical officers took a moment's break and walked outside for some fresh air.

The tactical uniforms used by SWAT teams are both practical and intimidating. Camouflage fatigues, black Kevlar helmets, face masks, and shatterproof goggles were topped off with a bristling array of semi-automatic weapons and numerous other weapons and tools that filled their multi-pocketed tactical vests. These were men ready to undertake a potentially dangerous mission, and they looked the part.

A loud noise attracted the attention of the team as a motorcycle suddenly rounded the corner of the station parking lot, driven by a husky young white man. The driver wore no helmet, which was a direct violation of the law. The bike rolled to a stop right in front of the seven members of the slightly surprised SWAT team.

The man turned off the bike's engine and addressed the officers with a loud and definitely intoxicated drawl.

"Say, fellers, can you tell me how to git to Smith's Body Shop?"

The Sergeant commanding the SWAT team stepped forward with a wry grin. "Sure, we can tell you how to get there. But I think you might be a little too drunk to be driving. What's your name?"

The man's demeanor became sharp as he glared at the Sergeant and stumbled off of the motorcycle.

"I'm 'The Rock,' if it's any of your business," snapped the man, referring to the pro wrestler by that name.

"Yeah, right," the Sergeant shot back, "and I'm 'Stone Cold.'"

"I reckon you're a smart-alec," said the man with a snarl, " and I might just have to whip you all over this parking lot." To the surprise of everyone, the man lunged for the Sergeant. It was as if he suddenly was blind to the fact that he was drunk, and driving, at a police station, not to mention threatening an already edgy and armed group of tactical officers. It only took a split second for the officers' shock to turn to anger.

"Get him!" somebody yelled. In a flurry of knees, elbows, boots, and camouflage, the drunk was quickly covered in SWAT team and on the pavement. He seemed still not to realize his mistake as he continued to curse belligerently as he was handcuffed and carried into the jail for booking.

The SWAT team returned to the office, dusting off their uniforms and equipment. By now, the whole episode had become somewhat humorous. Especially the man's reference to himself as "The Rock." It was clear that the man's mindless actions betrayed his impaired judgment and level of intoxication, and certainly kept him from being "Stone Cold."

Stone Cold sober, that is.

The Rain Was the Best Part of the Day

All day, it had rained. Creeks had risen and roads were wet with several inches of water. But the deputy had somehow managed to keep himself dry for his entire shift. His long yellow raincoat had been his constant companion all day, and although he had gone to several wrecks, domestic calls, and even a downed tree blocking a roadway, his uniform still looked as clean and fresh as it had that morning.

His dispatcher called out his unit number and instructed him to proceed to a rural area to where a woman was asking to speak with an officer. He acknowledged the call and drove in the direction of the residence. He'd stayed dry almost to the end of his shift, and this call would probably be an easy one. He noticed that even the rain seemed to be slacking up.

In fact, it had stopped raining entirely as he stopped in front of the small white house. For the first time all day, he left his raincoat in the front seat and walked casually up to the door. A slim woman invited him into the house, where in the front room he saw another heavy-set woman sitting near an old man in a wheelchair. The officer asked politely how he could help them.

"All I want is for my sister to leave," said the slim woman. "She more or less forced her way in my house, and now she won't leave."

"I see," answered the officer, looking to the other woman. "Is this true, ma'am?"

"She's trying to keep me away from my daddy," said the heavy woman sharply. "And I'm not leaving without him."

"I've been awarded custody and care of our father," said the slim woman, handing the deputy a court order. He glanced over the document, and noticed that the old man seemed to be mumbling something to himself, unaware of what was going on around him.

"Well," said the officer to the other woman. "I'm afraid your sister is right. I'm going to have to ask you to leave."

"I'm not leaving," said the woman quickly. "She can't keep me from seeing him."

"I'm sorry, but that's something the courts have to decide," the officer said. "But you are trespassing, and you have to leave."

"No, I'm not," she said.

For several minutes, the deputy tried to reason with the woman, but to no avail. No matter how much he tried, the lady refused to go peacefully. His patience began to leave him, and he began to grow angry.

"Look, ma'am. I've tried to ask you nicely. But if you don't go right now, then I'll be forced to escort you outside myself. And if you keep on, I'll have to arrest you"

"I'm not going," she snapped.

"Alright, then," he said, taking her by the arm. She immediately began to resist him, but he managed to pull her to her feet and lead her toward the door. The way the call had deteriorated so far had caused him to become quite frustrated, but his heart sank further when he opened the door and saw that the rain had resumed in full force. Hoping to get her outside and across the yard to her car as quickly as possible, he led her off the porch into the wet yard.

But a quick and clean end to the situation was not to be.

As the officer led the woman across the soggy grass, she began to resist him more forcefully. He ordered her to stop, but she continued to pull away and refuse to go.

"Fine," growled the deputy as he reached for his handcuffs. "Then I'm placing you under arrest." But as he did, the woman tugged away harder than before. Suddenly, they were both slipping over the wet grass, and the officer groaned as they fell with a plop into the grass and mud.

Struggling onto his feet, the officer tried to call on his radio for backup, but could not obtain a good transmission. He managed to place one of the handcuffs on the woman but could not seem to catch hold of her other flailing arm. He was trying not to harm the woman, but his options were dwindling. All over the wet ground they skated, and once again the deputy felt his feet sliding out from under him.

The officer lost his balance and landed flat on his back, with the woman tripping as well and landing directly on his chest.

Spitting out grass and mud, the officer felt as if his eyes were about to pop out of his head.

"You're hurting me," complained the woman as she rolled off of him.

"You're not the one getting fell on!" replied the deputy.

Finally, the officer was able to drag the woman over and pin her against the hood of his patrol car in order to lock the other handcuff. He placed her into the rear of the car just as other officers, who had heard his broken plea over the radio, began to arrive. Seeing their fellow officer's normally cleaned and pressed uniform covered in mud from head to toe was quite a sight.

"You boys got here just in time," said the deputy cynically. "I could have used some help getting to my rain coat."

Did You Say What I Think You Just Said?

The State Trooper had been working the interstate all afternoon and was ready for a break. It had been an unseasonably warm winter day, and his thirst for a good, cold, sugary fountain drink was overwhelming. Passing by a nearby convenience store, he saw that a clerk he knew was working. And since no other cars were in the parking lot, he thought he might enjoy some friendly conversation.

After filling up his icy drink, the Trooper stood alongside the counter talking casually with the clerk. After a few minutes, a small car driven by a young girl pulled up to the front door near his patrol car. It was plain to see that she was alone as she got out and entered the store.

With the Trooper standing beside the counter, the young girl approached the clerk and handed her a small card.

"I need some cigarettes," she stated. "This is all the ID I have."

The clerk looked at the card, which was only a social security card. "I'm sorry, but in order for me to sell you cigarettes, I have to see a picture ID with your birthday on it to show that you are at least eighteen. You know, like a driver's license."

"Well, I don't have a driver's license," said the girl casually. "But I'm twenty-two. So, I'm legal."

The clerk's eyes widened at the statement, and she glanced over at the Trooper still standing beside her at the counter. "Well, Miss, I still have to see a picture ID to sell you cigarettes."

The young girl seemed to grow impatient, placing her hands on her hips and speaking sharply to the clerk, never looking at the uniformed officer.

"All I want are some cigarettes."

"But I need some proper ID."

"I don't have a driver's license."

"Yes, That's what you said."

"Look, I'm over eighteen." The girl declared. "I'm twenty-two. Do you think I would just come in here in lie about it?"

"I still need to see a picture ID," repeated the clerk.

"But I don't have a driver's license!" exclaimed the girl once more. The Trooper nonchalantly leaned over and looked outside at the girl's car. The clerk began to grow amused.

"Ma'am, I'm real sorry," she said with a grin. "But state law prohibits me from selling anyone cigarettes without a picture ID, no matter how old they say they are."

"This is so stupid," hissed the girl, turning toward the door. "All I want is a pack of cigarettes."

The Trooper couldn't hold back any longer.

"Excuse me, Miss," he said with a friendly tone. "But did I just hear you correctly?"

"What do you mean?"

"I mean, did you say you didn't have a driver's license?"

The girl rolled her eyes as if she was growing tired of repeating herself.

"No. I don't have a driver's license."

"Well, then," said the Trooper, "Didn't I just watch you drive up to this store in that car out there?"

Maybe it was the girl's determination to boldly declare her age in order to buy a pack of smokes that caused her not to notice what she was admitting, but as she looked from the Trooper to the clerk, an extremely uncomfortable look came over her. She smiled weakly, her previous courage gone.

"Um, well, yeah I guess so."

"And you realize, of course, that I could arrest you and have your car towed away."

The girl simply nodded.

"But I'll tell you what," began the Trooper. "Rather than arrest you, tow your car, and have you stand in front of a judge while I relate the story of what I just saw and what you just said in front of me and a witness, I think you'd be better off just going over to that pay phone out there and calling someone to come and pick you up and drive your car home. What do you think?"

"I think I'll call somebody," she said softly.

"That's probably best," agreed the State Trooper. The girl turned and slunk out the door of the convenience store. As she did so, she mumbled something under her breath.

"Now I *really* need a cigarette."

Adapt and Overcome

"Unit 12, can you respond to Highway 613 South to a report of a mother having problems with her mentally-ill son?"

"10-4," answered the deputy glumly. Calls like this were always strange and difficult. People with mental illness were no different than any other citizens, but sometimes their own family members unintentionally caused problems. As he drove toward the call, he heard Unit 14 advise that he would be enroute also.

Upon their arrival, the officers walked up to a single story ranch-style house where a woman was waiting for them outside.

"It's my son," she said, "he's not been taking his medication like he's supposed to, and he's not acting right. I don't know what to do."

"Alright, ma'am," said the first deputy, hiding his dread. "We'll try to talk to him and calm him down."

They entered the home to find a slim, clean-shaven young man in his mid-twenties sitting on the couch in the living room. He was watching the television very closely, although it was turned off, and there was no picture on the screen. In his hands, he held a hot cup of coffee.

"Hey, there," said the second officer with a friendly smile.

"Hello," replied the young man. He took a large gulp of the hot liquid. "Are you here to arrest her?"

The officers looked at each other. "Arrest who?"

"Are you here to arrest my mother?" asked the man.

"Why would we want to arrest her?"

"Well, she's trying to kill me!" he said with a snort.

"How is she trying to kill you?"

"With poisoned bologna sandwiches," he said. "She's all the time trying to get me to eat poison bologna."

The deputies looked at each other again with raised eyebrows. "Well, okay then, would you like us to talk to her about that? Would that make you feel better?"

Suddenly the man stood up, causing the officers to step back cautiously. "I gotta get another cup of coffee. You guys want some?"

"Uh, no thanks, buddy," said the second officer, "but I think I'll go with you while you get some." The man walked out of the room with the officer in tow. They went into the kitchen, and the deputy watched as the man picked up the empty coffee pot and stared at it.

"Looks like you're out." The deputy stated.

"No, I'm not!" said the man with a laugh, at which point he replaced the pot inside the coffee maker and filled it with steaming hot water. The deputy watched in disbelief as the man poured himself a cup of the water and proceeded to down it as if it were iced tea on a hot day.

"That's good stuff," said the young man, who poured himself another cup and returned to the living room.

The deputy whispered to his partner what he had observed in the kitchen, and both men knew that something had to be done to calm the troubled man down, who was again staring at the blank television, taking large gulps of hot water.

"Say there," said the first officer, "have you been taking your pills that the doctor gave you?"

"I can't take them," answered the young man in exasperation. "The aliens won't let me."

"Oh, boy," said the second officer, rubbing his eyes.

"Where are these aliens at?" asked the first officer.

"Why, in outer space, of course!" said the man. "But they're sending messages to me through the television."

The deputy stepped over to the TV. "Right here? Is this where they are sending you messages?"

"Yep, right there."

"If I can stop the messages from coming, would you take your pills?"

"Sure I would!" exclaimed the man, taking another sup of scalding water. "Do you think you can do it?"

The deputy reached around and removed the expandable baton that was held in a holster behind his firearm. He gently extended the metal rod to its full length of 24 inches. "You see this? This is a tool we use to disrupt radio waves. Like the kind of radio waves that those aliens are sending you."

"Really?" said the man, his eyes wide with wonder.

"Now, watch this," added the deputy. As his partner attempted to control his laughter, the deputy waved the baton over the top and up the sides of the TV like a magic wand. With a look of serious concentration, he also passed it over the back of the set, saying, "This is usually where the radio waves come in."

After a few minutes of work, he officer stood up and closed the baton. "There now. That should do it."

After the man had taken his prescriptions, his mother thanked the officers for talking with her son. The young man was no less thankful to the deputies for using their skills to remove the alien messages.

"You know," the second officer joked as they walked back to their patrol cars, "I don't think I was ever taught that these batons we carry had so many special uses."

"Sometimes we must adapt and overcome, my friend," his partner replied. "Adapt and overcome."

Sometimes a Shotgun is Just a Shotgun

The headline of the Knoxville News-Sentinel read, "Man gets 27 months for having sawed-off shotgun." It grabbed my attention immediately. My first thought was that it seemed odd for someone to be given such a hefty sentence for simply possessing an illegal firearm. But then I remembered something that I have told a lot of people over the years: *you are not normally ever going to be caught with a firearm unless you are doing something you shouldn't be. And then, you usually deserve to be caught.* So, being the inquisitive gun owner that I am, I read on.

Yes, it was true. This poor unfortunate man, named Brian Keith McFarland, had indeed been charged with possessing an illegal sawed-off shotgun. The law states that a shotgun must have an overall length of 26 inches, with a barrel length of no less than 18 inches. Mr. McFarland's weapon had an overall length of 24 1/2 inches and a barrel length of 12 inches. Short on both counts, it seems. Definitely a dangerous and illegal firearm, but what were the circumstances that allowed Mr. McFarland to be caught?

Well, first of all, Mr. McFarland had been convicted before. In 1981 he was convicted of simple sexual assault, in 1982 he was convicted of carrying a weapon with intent to go armed, and in 1988 he received an indecent exposure conviction. You see, Mr. Brian McFarland is a sex offender with an apparent fondness for firearms. "Fondness" might not even be the strongest way to put just how Mr. McFarland feels about his guns, especially his illegal sawed-off shotgun.

How was Mr. McFarland caught? In May of 1999, three women in Knox County found photographs of Mr. McFarland on their car windshields. In the pictures he was completely nude, and holding (you guessed it) his sawed-off shotgun. He was convicted in July 1999 for Unlawful Production and Distribution of Obscene Matter, which of course led to his ultimate conviction for possession of the illegal weapon.

His defense was that the weapon was simply a "piece of art" and that "it ain't nothing but something to look at." Even though he claimed that the weapon would not work, agents with the ATF tested it and found that it would indeed fire.

Indeed, Mr. Brian McFarland makes responsible gun owners like myself proud to call him one of our own. About as proud as we could be about an illegal-gun-toting sex offender, that is. Incidents like this are fodder for those who would deny others the right to legally own firearms, which is yet another favor that Mr. McFarland has done for us.

But that is to be expected from someone of Mr. McFarland's caliber. I wonder what was going through his mind as the pictures were snapping.

You know, I really want to impress these girls. So, I think I'll leave them some pictures of me nude. Let's see what could I use to spice up these here pictures? Hey! I know! I'll hold this here little short, sawed-off shotgun that doesn't work! That will really impress them!

Paging Dr. Freud... Dr. Freud...

Please Don't Make Me Shoot That Dog

Probably one of the most requested calls for police officers, especially those in rural areas, is to respond to an animal call. Whether it is a "cow in the roadway," "mean-looking dog," or "snake in the house," officers must sometimes play the role of safari guide or trapper. But perhaps the least enjoyable type of animal call is when an officer is asked to "put down an animal."

And so it was one spring day, when an officer went to a house and spoke with a mother and her two small children. Their family dog, a cocker spaniel, had been hit by a car that morning and was badly hurt and suffering terribly. Would the officer please shoot the dog, the woman asked, in order to end its pain?

Looking into the tearful eyes of the children, the officer tried to think of some way to get out of this.

" I'd really rather not," he said. "Are you sure you don't want to take it to the vet?"

"I'm sure," she said, "He's too badly hurt and tries to bite me when I pick him up. There's nothing else to do."

Glancing at the children again, the officer tried one last time. "Ma'am, I just really hate to do something like this."

"Please?" she asked. "Even the kids understand that it has to be done." The officer watched as the two little children nodded hesitantly. Wishing he were somewhere else, he called his supervisor and told him what the woman was asking. The senior officer told him that as long as the pet owner was in agreement, he could use his firearm to put down the dog.

The officer finally agreed, and asked the woman if she would please take the children inside. They waved goodbye to their dog as their mother closed the door behind them. The officer took a deep breath and walked over to the edge of the yard to where the animal lay. He drew his weapon, pointed it at the dog, and fired.

To the officer's surprise and horror, the dog immediately began to yelp and drag itself across the grass. Embarrassed, the officer walked closer to the animal, aimed, and fired a second shot at the now moving target.

Perhaps it was his nervousness from knowing the dog still lived after the first shot that caused his second round to miss the dog entirely. As dirt flew up around him, the dog only yelped louder and crawled across the grass. The officer was further dismayed when he saw the two children standing in the window of their home, crying pitifully.

"I can't believe this," groaned the officer. Now almost sick and utterly humiliated at how the situation had worsened, he walked over to the dog once more. Steadying his hands, he took careful aim and fired a third time. At long last, the animal expired.

Holstering his weapon, he turned back to the house, fully expecting the family to berate him for causing prolonged suffering to their pet. To his surprise, the woman came outside and thanked him.

"I really do appreciate it," she said, "I know it must have been difficult."

"We know you really didn't want to shoot our dog," said the older of the two children. "We could tell you didn't want to."

"How could you tell that?" asked the officer.

"'Cause," said the child, "you were such a bad shot."

A Biting Duck Brings Out the Best In Everybody

I was, like most every other person, shocked when I read the story on the front page of the local paper. An innocent duck, shot and killed by an armed man, in one of Athens, Tennessee's, most peaceful and serene parks. The police had responded, of course, and had performed an intense and thorough investigation. The shooter, at last word, was going to claim self defense. A bloodthirsty and dangerous biting duck, as it were. It was one of those things that really makes a person think about what kind of a world we live in. I knew there had to be more to the story, so I went to the park to see the scene of the crime for myself.

I quickly found where the shooting had taken place. A few feathers lying about, some yellow crime scene tape hanging from the trees, the duck-shaped chalk outline still visible on the pavement. Nearby, a mother duck was grieving. Wishing to provide some comfort, I approached her.

"It was terrible," she said, as I threw her a handful of breadcrumbs. "He never had a chance."

She told me how he had grown up in a single duck home. His father had just up and "flown away" one night, she said. She had tried to raise him as best she could, but times were hard on a young and impressionable duck.

"To make matters worse, he was an ugly duckling," she said with a tear on her bill. "Except he never grew out of it."

She said that he was fairly well adjusted, and for some time, seemed to be like any other young duck. But then he started hanging out with the wrong crowd.

"He started swimming around with a group of wild geese," she told me. "I knew they were trouble, and I warned him and even begged him to stay away from them. He said for me not to worry, but I knew that something bad would happen.

"Then the biting started. At first, he denied he was doing it, but then he said it was no big deal. He claimed he was only biting a little on the weekends and at parties, but the habit began to take control of him. I tried everything to get him out of it, but he wouldn't listen."

Then, that fateful day came when he bit the wrong man. An armed man with an apparent fear of ducks.

"I was glad it was over as quick as it was," wept the mother duck. "You know, no flopping around like the chickens do."

As I was about to leave, she had nothing but compliments for the quick investigation performed by the Police Department.

"They were very kind, and I think they did an outstanding job. Situations like this are very hard on everyone. I think I even saw some of the officers get a little emotional. When the city workers took the body away, I could have sworn I heard one of them say something about dumplings, but I'm not sure what he meant."

As I left her there, waddling beside the water, my heart went out to her. It was a terrible thing to happen, that was for sure. But still one question was on my mind.

Are there any of those dumplings left?

I Know You Know I Know, But You're Lying Anyway

Living in a small, rural community has several advantages for a police officer. It is a world of "everybody knows everybody," and even if you aren't familiar with a particular person, you can bet you know someone who is. An officer is sometimes placed in a difficult position in having to arrest someone he grew up with or is related to, while at the same time, it is a benefit in being familiar with the person's background.

Once, on a roadblock on a hot summer day, I was assisting a group of fellow officers, drug agents, and district attorneys in stopping vehicles and checking for the drivers for DUI, expired or revoked licenses, or drugs if the stop involved an indication from the drug dog. After a few hours in the sun and angry comments from delayed drivers, we were thirsty, tired, and ready to be doing something else. It was about this time that an older model blue pickup truck came through the roadblock, and consequently it was I who held up my hand and asked the driver to stop.

The driver was a man in his early twenties, dressed in a ball cap, T-shirt, and blue jeans. The passenger was a slightly older and similarly dressed man. Both seemed a bit nervous as I leaned in the window to speak to them.

"Hello. This is a planned DUI and drug intervention roadblock. Could I see your identification please?" As I said the words, I immediately recognized the face of the driver. About fifteen years before, he and I had ridden the same school bus together. I knew him and his older brother well, as they lived basically in the same community as I did. He was several years younger than I was, and back then, I knew him as a funny little kid I enjoyed playing jokes on while riding the bus home. But even now, his face and voice were still the same. He had never been in any serious trouble, although I remembered seeing a warrant that had been issued for his arrest on failure to pay child support.

What surprised me at the roadblock was the fact that the name on the out-of-state driver's license he gave me was not his. I read the false information again and casually asked him his name.

"My name is Brad Smith," he said without hesitation. I knew his name wasn't Brad Smith. His name was Andy Evans. Curious, I played along. Calling my dispatcher, I ran the fake license, which came back valid with no history of violations.

"Well, Mr. Smith, would you please step out of your vehicle so I can speak with you?"

"Yeah, sure," he answered. We walked to the back of the truck, and I continued to quiz him.

"Mr. Smith, I'm not very familiar with driver's licenses from your state," I said, with a bit of untruth. "Could you recite to me the information on your license?"

As I listened, he recited the fake name, birthday, social security number, and address as if he were truly the person he claimed to be. I couldn't help but grin. He was good.

Had he been stopped by any of the other officers who were working the roadblock, "Brad Smith" would have passed right on through. No doubt he had performed the same Emmy-winning performance many other times when encountering police officers and had been successful each time. He had become so ingrained in his false impersonation that he felt confident he could fool anyone.

I thought to myself, "Is this guy stupid?" Common sense should tell you never to claim to be somebody else to a person who knows you.

After asking him his name for a third time (just to let him dig his hole a little bit deeper), I stepped close to him and said, "Listen. I don't know what you think you are trying to pull. I know who you are. You're not Brad Smith. You are Andy Evans. You and your brother Kyle rode my school bus. I know you like I know everybody that you and I grew up with. And you know me, too."

For an instant, he was about to insist that he was indeed Brad Smith. But his intent disappeared as he knew the jig was up. He lowered his head and shrugged. "Alright, you got me. Sorry about that."

As I arrested him on the outstanding warrant, he told me how he had gone to another state and obtained the driver's license, using his brother-in-law's information. His brother-in-law was mentally handicapped and had never been able to obtain his own license. The trick had worked. In his efforts to escape arrest, Andy Evans had become Brad Smith, and it had worked well for a couple of years.

So, rather than being arrested on the warrant, he was charged with Criminal Impersonation as well. On our way to the Justice Center, his voice was thick with disappointment.

"Of all the people I fooled with that ID, I had to get stopped by a guy I rode my school bus with."

It Wash the Besht Reashon Ever

The truck sped onward through the evening traffic, weaving in and out of the lanes and around the slower cars that moved closer to the legal speed limit. Even as he passed the black and white police car sitting with its radar gun pointing straight at him, the driver of the truck never slowed down. The police car gave a quick chase to the speeding truck, finally stopping him with blue lights and a few bursts of the siren as the truck approached the city limits.

The two officers got out of their vehicle and walked carefully up to the truck. They could plainly see the driver craning his neck around, angrily peering at the cops who had stopped him. The taller of the two police officers stepped to the driver's window.

"Hello, Sir. Do you know why we stopped you?"

"I don't really care why you shtopped me!" spat the middle-aged man behind the wheel. He tore his license from his wallet and threw it to the officer. "All I know ish you're nothing but a..." he proceeded to curse and swear at the officers in a way that would make a convict blush. At first, the officer thought the man's strange lisp was a sign he'd been drinking, but it became increasingly clear that the man was completely sober and was fuming mad.

"Now, hold on a minute, Sir," said the tall officer sternly. "You were traveling 66 miles per hour in a 45 mile per hour zone. You're 20 miles an hour over the limit. I think we have a right to pull you over."

"If you're going to write me a ticket, then jusht write it! I ain't got time to be lect-shured by shome two-bit roadshide flatfoot!" swore the man in a loud voice.

The tall officer gritted his teeth at the man's belligerence. He could have easily said more to the man, and it was all he could do to maintain an air of professionalism as he spun on his heel and walked back to the patrol car.

"What on earth did you say to that guy to get him ticked off like that?" laughed the other cop.

"Nothing!" cried the tall cop. "He never even gave me a chance to cut him a break!" He scribbled information onto the ticket book. "Man, what a jerk this guy is."

"Why is he so mad?"

"I have no idea. And I hate when people talk to me like that. I swear if I could arrest the guy, I'd throw him under the jail."

"Temper, temper," his partner teased. "Maybe he's got a good reason to be such a horse's tail."

The ticket completed, the officers stepped back up to the truck. The tall officer was beginning to feel a little satisfaction in giving the man a ticket, but the feeling disappeared when he faced the driver again. Sitting behind the truck, the man was quiet and forlorn, with tears streaming down his cheeks. The officers were taken aback.

"Is everything alright, Sir?" asked the tall cop.

The man shook his head. "No, not really, Shir. I shouldn't have shaid all that shtuff to you like I did. Thish ish all jusht a big mishtake."

"What do you mean?"

"Well, thatsh why I'm in shuch a hurry, and I shound sho funny. I'm trying to get back to Knoxshville becaush I left shomething up their today when I went to vishit my shishter."

The officer was curious. "What was it you left?"

The man looked the officer square in the eye and grinned a toothless smile. "My teethsh. I ran off and forgot my falsh teethsh."

The other cop turned away to hide his laughter as the tall officer stood there holding the ticket book with his mouth dangling open.

"Like I shaid, I'm shorry about looshing my temper," continued the man.

The tall cop just shook his head as he tore the ticket in half. "Sir, I've been doing this job a long time, and that's about the best excuse I've ever heard. I think I'll let you go with a warning this time."

"I really appreshiate that, offisher," said the man meekly as he drove away.

Watching the truck disappear down the road, the tall officer heard the voice of his partner behind him.

"That was sho shweet. He wash lucky you're shuch a nishe guy."

It Happens to Everybody. Doesn't It?

For most people, it will happen sometime over the course of their career. Their morning routine will become so commonplace that they will arrive at work not remembering that they have left some important item at home. And it will be at some crucial point during that day that the gut wrenching realization will come.

Sometimes, it may be something as inconsequential as a pair of eyeglasses or a cell phone. I even had a teacher in high school who was more than a little forgetful. She was rumored to have shown up for work one winter morning, and upon removing her overcoat, realized, along with her entire first period class, that she had forgotten to put on her skirt.

It is something that happens to the best of us. And for a police officer, who has to remember to bring to work with him a plethora of weapons, body armor, uniform attire, and paperwork, things can sometimes be forgotten. Especially when a safety-conscious officer like myself removes his weapon from his holster after his previous shift in order to unload it and store it in a secure location at home.

Running a little late for work one day, I quickly gathered up my things and drove off in my patrol car. As luck would have it, a call came out for an officer to respond to a report of threats being made. It was on my way in, so I took the call.

Sauntering up to the door of the residence, a woman came outside and told me how her ex-boyfriend had been calling her with threats of burning her house down. Just as I was about to respond with "Not while I'm around," I instinctively reached for the familiar and comforting handle of my .40 caliber handgun. All I felt in the holster was air. My heart sank into my boots. In my mind, I could plainly see my handgun, locked away safely in its box in my closet at home.

Trying to hide a combination of embarrassment, terror, and shock, I confidently advised the woman that she might be better off staying with a friend for a little while. The woman was painfully slow in gathering some personal items as I scanned the road for the approach of the boyfriend who might show up at any time and complicate matters even more. Finally she left, and I returned home as fast as the speed limit would let me to recover my wayward weapon.

I should say that I was, by far, not the only officer to occasionally forget such a necessary tool of the trade. It has happened, and continues to happen, to other cops who get in a little bit too much of a hurry to get to work. It's not something any officer likes to admit, especially not to another cop. But we're all human, and sometimes we simply have a lapse in memory. I'm just thankful that, unlike my high school teacher, no one ever actually saw me without my much needed weapon.

Thank goodness I never had to remember to put on a dress.

The Best Hiding Place Ever

"Oh, no! It's the cops!"

The woman at the window saw the approaching patrol cars gliding slowly up the driveway, and her declaration brought her boyfriend to his feet.

"Oh, man!" swore the lanky, bearded man. "Them warrants have been out for two weeks now. I knew it was just a matter of time." He looked frantically around the house, looking for a place to hide. "What am I gonna do?"

The blonde thought quickly as her red fingernails danced across the windowpane in front of her. "You gotta get out of here. Right now."

"Where can I go?" cried the wanted man. "They're almost here!"

"Just take off out the back door," she said. "They'll never see you. I'll hold them up long enough for you to get away. Now git!"

"Alright, baby," the man stole a quick kiss on her thickly coated red lipsticked lips. Without looking back, he dashed out the back door.

The woman watched as the two patrol cars came to a stop in front of her house, and four officers got out, walked up, and knocked on her door. She put on her best fake smile and answered the door with an innocent voice.

"Hello, officers, can I help you?"

"Yes ma'am, we think you can," said the tall officer with sandy-brown hair that was combed up, Elvis-like on top of his head. "We have an arrest warrant for Ricky Lee Jim Bob Luallen, Junior. Do you know him?"

The blonde woman gave the officer a wide-eyed look. "Yes, Ricky Lee's my ex. I ain't seen his sorry hide in about a week though. What's he done this time?" As she spoke, she pointed upward, toward her ceiling, nodding her head upward.

"Nothing serious, ma'am," said the slim cop, confused for a moment. "It's just a violation of probation charge. Do you mind if we come in and look for him?"

"Oh, no, not at all. But he ain't here," she said, continuing to gesture toward her ceiling. The officer began to nod his head and grin. He leaned toward her ear and whispered, "Attic?" She nodded with as serious a face as she could put on.

The officers, thinking they were being given good information, were completely hooked. They gleefully followed the devious blonde to a closet where she pointed to an access door.

The slim officer drew his weapon, and with some difficulty, crawled through the tight door, up into the attic. Another officer, not as tall as the sandy-brown Elvis, followed his partner up into the attic with a sneaky smirk.

The woman watched as the remaining two officers watched and listened intently for any signs of the capture they believed to be imminent. She smiled, thinking of how Ricky Lee Jim Bob Luallen, Junior, must surely be long gone by now.

It quickly became apparent that the attic space was rather cluttered and a bit too small for a tall cop. The sounds of stumbling feet, items falling, bumped heads, and assorted swearing drifted down from the cramped attic space. One of the officers standing by turned to the woman and whispered, "Are you sure he's up there?"

"Well," she said sweetly, "I think he might be."

"If he is, they'll get him," said the officer confidently. "Those guys are professionals."

It was at that moment that pieces of the ceiling came crashing down, followed by a long, skinny, uniformed leg that dangled weakly from the attic above.

"Ouch!" cried the tall cop with the Elvis hair. "Sorry about that, ma'am. Somebody get me out of here!" The other two officers scrambled over and pushed the leg back up into the attic. After a few more minutes of stumbling around, the two cops climbed back down, covered in dust.

"I don't think he's up there," grumbled the tall officer, pulling some old Christmas tinsel out of his hair. "We didn't see a thing."

"Hey!" yelled one of the other officers. "Look at this. The back door is open."

As the officers began to realize they had been duped, the blonde smiled one last fake smile as she lit a celebratory cigarette.

"My, my," she said ever so sweetly, "now that sure is strange."

These Feet Weren't Just Made for Walking

Stepping carefully to the door of the old farmhouse, the deputy knocked and waited. He'd been dispatched to the location with the report of a domestic disturbance between a mother and a son. He waited a few more seconds with no answer at the door, then he knocked again. A voice called out from the side of the house.

"He's out here!"

Walking around the corner, the deputy observed a plump older woman sitting in a lawn chair in the shade of a large tree. About ten feet in front of her stood a skinny man in his thirties, dressed in tattered blue jeans and a worn T-shirt. But the one thing that the officer noticed the most was the man's hair, which stuck up wildly all over his head. The man scowled at the officer as he walked close.

"Hello! What seems to be the trouble?"

"Bobby's been drinkin,'" said the woman, fanning herself with a rolled up newspaper. "I can't do nothin' with him when he's like this."

"Now, Bobby," began the deputy, hoping to calm the situation without anyone having to go to jail, "surely you're not giving your mama a hard time."

"I ain't doin' a thing," answered Bobby in a sharp but shaking voice. "She just won't let me be. And don't you think you're coming up here to take me to jail, either. 'Cause I'm a dangerous man." At that, Bobby assumed what appeared to be some sort of martial arts stance. He held out his arms like a buzzard, and with one leg extended, he began to kick at the officer. It was clear Bobby had been watching too many movies. It was also clear that Bobby had drank too much, because after he kicked two or three times, he began to wobble on the one leg. Losing his balance, he fell backward over another lawn chair. Reluctantly, the deputy handcuffed him and took him to jail.

In the two days he spent in jail, Bobby made few friends. To say his demeanor was a bit skewed would have been an understatement.

Other prisoners said he was "a few bricks shy of a full load." If not for his continuously antagonistic behavior, he had another problem: his feet stank. And not just a little bit. By the second night, other inmates were begging to be moved away from him. And no matter how much the corrections officers threatened him, Bobby refused to do anything about the smell. Still, there was something about the way he seemed to think the world revolved around him that caught the officers as humorous.

The day came for his appearance in court, and Bobby was transported with two other men to the courthouse. In an effort to alleviate his personal hygiene problem, his shoes had been taken away, and he'd been issued a pair of jail sandals. The two other prisoners found that the sandals didn't do much good and asked repeatedly for the transporting officer to roll down the windows.

The courtroom was still quite full when the judge called up Bobby's case. Bobby shuffled to the front of the room and stood at the bench beside his mother. As word of Bobby's behavior had gotten around, the police officers and deputies were watching to see what he would do. The judge read the arrest warrant.

"Bobby Blackwell, you're charged with disorderly conduct. How do you plead?"

"I ain't guilty, Sir."

"I see." The judge then addresses the woman. "And you are his mother?"

"I'm afraid so."

"Ma'am, the officer's report says that Bobby here was acting in a threatening manner and was drunk and disorderly toward both himself and you. Is that true?"

"Yes."

"Now, hold on a minute, Judge," declared an obviously incensed Bobby. "I don't reckon that's right."

"Bobby, if you'll just remain quiet—"

"Can I ask you somethin', Judge?"

"No, not right—"

"Well, this is what I want to ask you," continued Bobby, unabated. He propped himself up on the bench with one arm, appearing much like an un-casual man trying to look casual. "I want to know if you'll tell my Mama somethin'."

The judge rolled his eyes and resigned himself. "What's that, Bobby?"

"I want you to tell my Mama," declared Bobby, "that she ain't the boss of me."

The police officers and deputies standing nearby tried their best to control their giggling. Bobby gave his mother one of those 'I got you now' looks. The judge began to lose his patience.

"Look, Bobby," grumbled his Honor, " I'm going to find you guilty. All I can tell you is you'd better start getting along with your mother. Your sentence is suspended so long as you pay your fines and court costs. You're free to go once you get back to the jail."

Bobby's mother whispered some stern words to her son, who hung his head and shuffled out of the courtroom. It was all the cops could do to hide their laughter when the judge turned to the clerk beside him and asked, "Do you smell something?"

Smothered, Covered, and Scrambled, with Chili on It

For the police officer on the midnight shift, there are few places he can go to for a sit-down meal. Unlike day shift, restaurants and most fast food joints are closed overnight, so the officer's choices are limited. So it's not surprising to see patrol cars gathered around the all-night cafe/breakfast establishments like the Waffle House.

Not everybody is lucky enough to have had the Waffle House experience. Only those few people who regularly work or play during the late hours of the night know what an interesting place a Waffle House can be. It's a different breed of people. After all, it takes a real man to eat chili and wash it down with hot black coffee at 3:00 A.M.

And only a certain type of hard-nosed waitresses can stand the long hours of the midnight shift. She is normally over forty, a smoker, with a worn face from too many hours spent in a cramped and steamy environment. She will have a name like "Jean" or "Evelyn" or "Mavis." Mavis will be friendly and talkative, a lady who doesn't mind sharing little tidbits of her day with you, no matter how graphic those little tidbits may be.

"Hello, honey. You come on in and sit down. Whew! It's been one of them nights. Busy, busy. My back's about out and my corns are killing me. Now, what would you like to eat?"

Her honesty is disarming, and as she takes your order, she is pleasant and as sweet as your favorite aunt, the one you liked to be around but never liked to kiss. Your order scribbled down on the official Waffle House Order Note Pad, her demeanor changes suddenly as she turns and screams to the cook in some strange foreign language with a voice loud enough to rattle the silverware on the table, "Hey Jimmy! Got two smothered, chopped and chunky, on a well-done with a side of regular over-easy on dark with three strips and a Belgian!"

Hoping her directions have something to do with your order and not a European Terrorist Group, you settle in with what you can assume is a meeting of the Midnight Smokers' Association. Never go into a Waffle House and ask where the "non-smoking section" is. If you are not bodily removed from the building, the waitress is sure to give you a stern look and answer with a condescending tone, "Honey, I guess the 'non-smoking' section is whichever booth you decide to sit at."

But to never have been to the Waffle House is to miss the best part of the experience: the food. The food at the Waffle House is probably the best tasting and best priced, anywhere. It's not just good; it's great. As an officer, I've put away many servings of sirloin steak and eggs with a big syrup-covered waffle on the side, and a coffee cup that never seems to go empty. I never had bad service, and I never had bad food, and that is definitely a compliment when it's said about an all-night diner. It's probably one of my favorite places to eat.

And it's a good thing that the food is so good, because you won't find a place to complain about it, even if you wanted to. Which brings up my last bit of advice: *Never ask for the Complaint Department at the Waffle House.*

Mavis or Jean or Evelyn will give you a stern look and tell you it's located in the non-smoking section.

Blondes Have More Fun with Ambulances and Crayons

"Look," said the EMS Lieutenant, "you gotta understand. I've got nuthin' against women. It's just that this is the first time we've ever had two women working together on an ambulance before."

The two seasoned female paramedics listened with arms crossed and stern eyes that betrayed their offense at their supervisor's words. Both were experienced street veterans with clean records of service. Neither appreciated the lecture they'd had to endure at 7:00 A.M., just as their first shift together was about to start.

The Lieutenant rambled on, "You know, I gotta tell you both this, 'cause the brass is down on me if anything were to happen. They're still a little edgy after those guys wrecked the ambulance last month.

"Funny you should mention that, Chief," snapped the shorter of the two women, "because neither of us have ever wrecked an ambulance in all the years we've worked here."

"Yeah, yeah, I know," answered the nervous Lieutenant as he realized any more lecturing could cost him a body part. "You girls just be careful out there."

Watching him walk away, the short blonde Medic hissed. "Girls!? Did you hear what he said?!"

"Don't worry about him," said her tall, dark-haired partner. "He's probably got issues with his mother."

It was a winter day, gray and cold, with the temperature hovering around freezing. Although they had been anxious for some calls to come in, the two women found themselves lounging around the station for most of the morning. Feeling the need to grab something to eat, they hopped into their ambulance to enjoy a drive through town.

But, as luck would have it, a call came in to interrupt their dinner plans.

"907, be enroute to White Mountain Road. We've got an older gentleman needing a ride to the hospital."

"10-4" radioed the blonde driver. Her partner quickly scanned over their map book.

"I don't remember a White Mountain Road," she mumbled, "and I can't find it on the map. Do you know where we're going?"

"I know where it is."

"Are you sure?"

"Trust me!" answered the short woman. Her apparent overconfidence did not give her brunette partner a good feeling.

The road the driver found hung precariously to the side of a steep ridge. For miles, they drove the big rig around hairpin curves until the pavement gave way to gravel, then the gravel gave way to dirt. Plowing through an iced-over mud hole, the dark-haired Medic decided she'd had enough.

"I've had enough of this," she grumbled. "I think we're lost."

"I don't know. Maybe..." said the shorter woman as she steered the ambulance around a tight curve. After a mile or so more, she found a place to turn the large vehicle around and began making their way back down the mountain. Once more, they came upon the frozen mud hole.

But this time the mud hole was not so easy to pass through. The cold air had frozen the mud into a solid sheet of ice. Both women suddenly felt the ambulance start to slide.

"What are you doing?!" yelled the dark-haired Medic.

"Nothing!" her partner yelled back. "Just shut up and hold on!"

The ambulance began to spin gracefully on the ice, until it was literally traveling sideways down the road. No matter how the driver fought to regain control, the truck would not respond. Then both of their hearts stopped as the ambulance suddenly left the road and rolled forward down the side of the ridge.

Neither woman could speak as the rig bounced along through the trees. Just when they'd resigned themselves to certain death, the ambulance caught itself against two large trees that stopped its slalom run down the hillside.

For a few minutes, the two women sat frozen in their seats, trembling. Then, almost at once, they began to laugh. They laughed until they cried.

"They did everything they could," said the traffic cop to the

Lieutenant. "It's this weather that caused it. They're lucky, though. Could have been a whole lot worse."

"Well, at least you girls are all right." sighed the Lieutenant, turning to the two female Paramedics warming themselves in the back of the cop car. "But I'll need statements from both of you."

"Here's your statement," snapped the tall brunette as she tossed him a folded traffic accident report form she'd found in the cop car. "This should be appropriate, since you've been treating us like kids all day."

The Medics were driven away as the Lieutenant opened the report. The bitter women had filled out the entire report, complete with an accident diagram showing a cartoon-like ambulance bouncing down the hill.

The report had been written with a bright red crayon.

Drunks and Cops

One of the more bittersweet aspects of police work is dealing with drunks. A "drunk" can be any intoxicated person that officers encounter on the streets, but to most officers, a drunk is someone who the officer knows all too well. It may sound odd, but sometimes a relationship can develop between cops and "drunks," sort of like Andy and Otis on "The Andy Griffin Show."

When a person develops an addiction to alcohol that is so severe that all other desires of life are left behind in pursuit of the next drink, they become, at least in a police officer's eyes, a "drunk." They are those poor souls who generally are not violent, never harm anyone (except sometimes each other), and are actually pretty decent old guys deep down inside. While the label may sound harsh, it really isn't, especially when officers and drunks get to know each other after several years of numerous encounters. Many times, a certain amount of affection, even strange friendships, can develop.

Sometimes, they even earn nicknames from the police who deal with them, like "Suds," "P-Sam," and "Roadrunner." Fellows like these are often found on the wrong end of a bottle, and found that way almost all the time. But after a while, police officers develop a sense of pity for these guys. Arrest is usually the last option an officer will use, especially after the person has been arrested numerous times with no change in their behavior. Sometimes a simple ride home would keep the man out of trouble (and sometimes danger), and when a "drunk" knows he can trust an officer he will be much more likely to stay home and "sleep it off."

Some of these men come to accept their affliction of alcoholism, even to the extent of developing a sense of humor about it. Once, an officer was out on patrol when he came upon a "drunk" he knew well. The man was walking down the road carrying a plastic grocery bag, and seeming to be more sober than usual. The officer pulled alongside and offered the man a ride.

With an uncertain look in his eye, the man replied, "You ain't gonna take me to jail are you?"

"Of course not!" said the officer. "You've not done anything wrong have you?"

"No, I guess not," answered the man after a few seconds of consideration. Then, with a devious look in his eye, the man asked, "Say, can I drink me a few beers while you take me home? I've always wanted to drink beer in a cop car."

The officer, of course, declined the man's request, and though a little disappointed, the man accepted the ride home nevertheless.

Some of these men have tragic backgrounds. Some are homeless. Others have college degrees. Some are veterans, even decorated war heroes. Others experienced some tragic event in their lives that drove them over the edge and into a bottle. Every now and then, officers get to know a "drunk" who exhibits a tremendous amount of intellect.

For example, there was once an old fellow who was known quite well among officers as a "drunk." He never gave anyone any trouble and always seemed genuinely interested in a police officer's job. The large amount of time he spent dealing with cops wound up providing him with a lot of information concerning laws and their enforcement. It was knowledge that he was able to put to good use.

One day, the man spied an old police uniform at a yard sale. Obtaining his bargain, he immediately went home, cleaned himself up, and put on the uniform. Later that night, he found a big party going on at a nearby lake. With the festivities in high gear, the man walked in and declared he was the police. He claimed he'd received several complaints about the ongoing party, and he was going to have to take some action. The gullible and intoxicated partygoers watched as the "officer" gave them a strong warning as to what might happen if they didn't calm the party down. Then, before he left, he thanked them for their cooperation and did what officers are supposed to do in such a situation: He happily confiscated all of their beer. It was a case where one "drunk" out-smarted several drunks.

After all, you can't argue with the "police."

Cops Don't Just Make Mistakes....

Far be it from me to ever say that cops are perfect. Although there is a large amount of "a polished image" associated with police officers, they are merely people underneath those uniforms. And although I hate to admit it, cops make mistakes just like anybody else.

No, I take that back. When cops make mistakes, they make huge ones.

Being a cop can be a difficult and stressful job. But it's not all bravado and courage like is implied on shows like "COPS." In fact, bravado can quickly turn to overconfidence, which can lead to stupidity, which can get you killed. Take for example an incident that occurred in a nearby county. Deputies there picked up a man walking along the interstate who was acting a bit strange. Thinking he might need a mental evaluation, one of the officers transported the man to the nearest hospital emergency room.

The man happened to be carrying a backpack. Although I'm not quite sure why he did it, the deputy allowed the man to keep the backpack with him while he rode in the police car to the hospital. The officer did not even bother to search the bag. Once at the hospital, the man became distraught and asked to go to the restroom. There he took a knife out of his backpack and injured himself severely. Only then did police find the numerous knives and even some ammunition for a firearm inside his bag. The deputy who brought him in could have easily been killed simply because he failed to search the man's bag or at least keep it out of reach of the man until the situation was found to be safe.

Escorting funerals can sometimes turn ugly. For departments who still perform such a service, the officer must be as sensitive and respectful as he can to the grieving family. After all, the officer is leading family and friends on a loved one's last ride to their final resting place.

One bright sunny day, such a cop was leading a funeral procession down a highway, when, for some unknown reason, he took a wrong turn.

His partner who was riding with him started yelling, "You're going the wrong way!" The officer suddenly panicked when he realized his mistake.

"Ohmygosh! Where does this road come out at? Can we get to the cemetery from here!?"

"I don't know!" screamed his partner. "I think this might be a dead end!"

"What are we gonna do!?"

The second officer glanced back at the long line of cars that were now following them down the wrong road. He covered his face with his hands and slid down in the front seat, groaning, "I can't believe you did this."

"OK! OK!" yelled the first officer, trying to calm himself down, and trying to remember where the road led. "I think we might be able to get back over to the highway." He gently, slowed the patrol car to a stop and opened his door.

"What are you doing?!" screamed his partner.

"Just trust me!" The officer walked back to the hearse, where the confused funeral director met him with a bewildered look.

"We had to take a side road," said the deputy quickly, with a fake tone of confidence. "There was, ah, a wreck, yeah! Um, we thought there was a wreck, but there's not, so just follow us." The officer spun around and got back into the patrol car.

"I sure hope you're right about this," said the partner, "because if you're not, we're probably gonna get fired."

But luck was on the side of the inattentive cop, and he was able to lead the lost procession back onto the highway and on to their "final destination."

Blue lights can also lead to embarrassing mistakes. I recall several years ago while working as a patrol officer, I turned on my blue lights to stop another car for a traffic violation. After releasing the driver, I continued my patrol duties, slowly cruising the streets and back roads. As I drove along, I noticed that people seemed to be eager to get out of my way as I drove up behind them, some even pulling over to let me pass. I considered this to be very polite, so I would smile and wave to the drivers as I casually went slowly around them. I also noticed that people standing in their yards seemed to be paying a lot of attention to me as I drove by. I felt pretty good, people seemed to be unusually interested in my job. Finally, I passed another officer who radioed me on the private channel.

"Dude," he giggled," you're driving around with your blue lights on."

I looked down and saw that indeed I had forgotten to turn them off after the traffic stop. I gingerly reached down and flipped the switch, waving weakly to the fellow officer who was laughing so hard he could barely drive. I imagined the people I'd passed, wondering what in the world I was doing slowly driving around with my emergency lights on, waving and smiling like a homecoming queen. I assume they were thinking some pretty crazy things.

That deputy must have somewhere important to go, but he sure ain't in no hurry to get there.

Till Theft Do Us Part

The bonds of marriage are some of the strongest attachments a man and woman may experience together. It is a solemn and precious moment when two people stand before God, their families, and their friends and make the holiest of commitments to each other: to "love, honor, and cherish each other till death do us part." Such touching and heartfelt devotion between two consenting adults can surely never be broken for the rest of their lives, right?

Well, sometimes...

The detective's telephone rang as he was browsing over the last week's burglary reports. Shuffling through the pile of paper, he picked up the phone and answered.

"Detective division."

The female voice at the other end of the line was soft and somewhat hesitant. "Is this a detective?"

"Yes, ma'am," he answered. "You're speaking with a detective."

"OK," she said. "Then I have some information for you."

"What kind of information?" he said.

"It's about a burglary."

The detective continued to dig through the stack of papers in front of him, only somewhat attentive to what the woman was saying. He received a lot of calls like this, which usually turned out to be of no relevance to a crime. Usually it was just someone being suspicious of someone else, with no solid proof to back up the accusation.

"I'm listening," he said.

"It's about the Waldorf burglary," she said. " I know where all of the guns are."

Suddenly, the detective sat up. Very quickly, he looked back through the reports until he found the one he'd seen earlier, one which had been taken at the Waldorf residence. He examined the lengthy list of firearms that had been stolen, and his attention became focused on the woman's information.

"Yes," he said, "I'm familiar with that report. So where do you think those guns are at?"

"I don't think," she declared. "I know exactly where they are hidden."

"Can you tell me where?"

"They're in my husband's closet." She said matter-of-factly.

The detective leaned back in his chair. "Well, I suppose I need to come over and check the serial numbers on the guns, just to be sure they are the right ones."

"Oh, they are the right guns all right. I know they are."

"How can you be sure?" he asked.

"Because I was over at Mr. Waldorf's house when he reported them stolen. I was there when the officers came after the burglary was found."

The detective was intrigued, so he naturally asked, "Ma'am, what were you doing over at Mr. Waldorf's house?"

The woman's voice became quiet for a moment. "Well, I've been spending quite a bit of time at Mr. Waldorf's house over the past few months, if you know what I mean."

The detective's eyes widened as he realized exactly what she meant. "Oooooohhhh. I see. So let me get this straight. You are having an affair with Mr. Waldorf, and it just so happens that you were there when the guns were found stolen, and now you've found them in your husband's closet, and you've called to tell me all about it."

"Yes, that's right."

Somewhat shocked, but still hoping to solve the burglary, the detective said, "Well, ma'am, I suppose I'd better come out to your home and talk to your husband."

"Alright," She replied. "But if you don't mind, please don't tell my husband I told you all of this. I don't want him to be disappointed in me."

The detective arrived at the house, and after examining the guns that were in the husband's closet, he placed the surprised man under arrest and secured him in the back of a police car. After taking a statement from the wife, the man was taken to the jail to be booked.

After the booking process was completed, the husband was allowed to call someone to post bail for his release. The first number the clueless man dialed was, of course, that of his loving and devoted wife.

He was surprised when no one answered the phone.

You've Never Heard a Hearing Like This

The courtroom had seen its normal lineup of daily cases pass through, and the judge was about to begin what would be the last action of his day. Several hearings were scheduled to complete the daily docket, and the Judge was anxious to get them over with. After all, the fish were biting, and he was ready to get an early start on his weekend.

As he looked over the docket, he noticed a name on his list. He peered over the bench to look out over the crowd seated in the courtroom and recognized her immediately. She was a skinny woman with wild hair and was well known among police officers and social workers. A long history of psychosis had plagued her for many years. As long as she took her medicine, she rarely had any problems. But when she did not, she would develop a strange and distant look in her eyes and was prone to extremely bizarre behavior. It was the same look that the judge saw now, and he knew he'd better go ahead and hear her case before she did or said anything to disrupt his court.

"Let's hear this case first," he told the District Attorney.

The DA glanced over the file and wrinkled her nose. "Are you sure about that?"

"Absolutely," said the Judge. "She's probably already tired of waiting all morning. I don't want her to get too distressed."

"You're the Judge," sang the DA as His Honor called out the woman's case.

She stood up like a rocket, walked, spider-like, to the front of the courtroom, and stood at a crooked angle before the Judge. Here eyes were wide and wild, and she murmured to herself under her breath. From a large table at the left of the courtroom, a police officer stood up as well. Both were sworn to testify, to which the woman croaked an unintelligible response along with the deputy's " I do."

"Are you the arresting officer?" began the DA.

"Yes." Replied the young man.

"I see you've charged the defendant with Indecent Exposure. Can you tell the court what exactly happened?"

The officer glanced at the Judge, obviously a little uncomfortable. "I can, if you really want me to do that."

"Of course we want you to do that," interjected the Judge. "So, go ahead with your testimony."

The officer swallowed nervously. "Yes, Your Honor. You see, I was coming back from lunch that day in my patrol car, going back to the station...."

"So, it was during the day?" asked the DA.

"Yes, about noon," replied the officer. "It was a sunny day, warm. There were a lot of people out, a lot of cars on the road. Anyway, I was coming up the main highway when I saw her."

"The defendant?"

"Yes," he nodded.

"And where was the defendant when you saw her?"

"She was in the middle of the road, in the middle of the four-lane highway."

"And what was the defendant doing?"

"She had her dress pulled up."

The DA's eyes widened, and the Judge sat up to peer over the bench. The woman stood in the same spot, still fidgeting and murmuring to herself.

"I see..." said the DA, then she asked very slowly, "And what was she doing with her dress pulled up?"

The police officer shifted his weight from one foot to the other, his neck and face bright red. "She was, ah, well, she was, you know, 'going to the bathroom.'"

For a moment, the DA stood very still, her mouth gaping open. The Judge's chair creaked as he leaned further forward to make sure he was understanding everything. Not a word was spoken in the courtroom. The woman continued to talk to herself. The officer hoped he was not about to be held in contempt.

"Now let me get this straight," the DA said. "You drove up and saw the defendant in the middle of the highway with cars all around, and she was clearly...you say she was..."

"Yes, that's what she was doing," answered the officer, blurting out his own defense. "I had to stop, because there were cars everywhere, and everybody was looking at me, you know, like they expected me to do something After all, I am the police, and so I had to do something...."

"Of course you did," agreed the DA. "And what was it you did?"

"I just stopped my patrol car," he said, "And she came running over and opened the back door and jumped in the rear seat."

"Did she say anything?" asked the DA.

"She kept yelling, 'Take me to jail for indecent exposure! Take me to jail for indecent exposure!'"

The DA, like everyone else in the room, was bewildered at the officer's tale. "And what did you do then?"

"I slammed that patrol car into drive and tore off to the jail as fast as I could get out of there."

The Judge slammed the gavel onto the bench. "That's enough. I think we all get the picture." Then he addressed the woman. "I'm finding you guilty, but consider your sentence suspended with time already served when you were brought in, so long as you get back on your medication and stay out of trouble. You're free to go."

The woman looked at the Judge with her wild eyes. She shrugged one crooked shoulder and walked stiffly out of the courtroom, grumbling words that only she could understand.

The DA leaned over to the Judge. "You went pretty easy on her after all that."

"Like I said before, she's been waiting all morning," sighed the Judge, "and I figured it was about time I let her go to the bathroom."

I'm Ready to Go to Jail Now, I Think

Driving slowly through the parking lot of the truck stop, the two deputies scanned the rows of parked tractor-trailers. Prostitutes and petty thieves often worked truck stops such as this one, for here they found easy prey among men and women who traveled the highways. Not much had happened during their shift, and the officers were anxious to find something to "get into." But nevertheless, the rows of quietly idling semis were devoid of any criminal activity. So the officers simply parked out in front of the truck stop to relax.

They had been chatting for a few minutes when the back door of the patrol car suddenly opened. Both young men were startled as a thickly built, middle-aged man with a beard plopped down into the seat behind them and shut the door.

"What do you think you're doing?" yelled the officer who was driving.

"I need to go to jail," said the man, his words slurred and his eyes glassy.

"Say what?" cried the other officer, still a little uneasy at the sudden invasion of their patrol car.

"Take me to jail," repeated the big man, "I'm drunk." Both officers caught the fruity smell of alcohol on the man's breath.

"You can't just sit down in here like this!" said the first officer.

"Why not?"

"Because…," stammered the young officer, unsure of his answer. "Because you just can't. That's not the way it works!"

"Well, I don't care how it works," continued the man. "I'm drunk, and I need to go to jail."

Unfortunately for the intoxicated man, he had decided to turn himself in to two rookie officers, who, although they had been intent on "getting into something" a few minutes before, were now very unsure exactly what to do. So, since the man refused to get out of the car, they got out themselves. Standing beside the patrol car, they tried to decide on the right course of action.

"What are we gonna do?" asked the second deputy.

"I don't know," shrugged the first deputy, "Maybe we should probably give him a sobriety test." He opened the back door and ordered the man to get out.

"Nope," he refused, "I ain't gettin' out. Take me to jail."

The officers reached in to pull the man out, but he fought them off. There seemed to be no way to remove him from the car.

The second deputy's level of frustration had finally overtaken him. "Forget this," he hissed, "I'm calling the sergeant."

About ten minutes later, the patrol sergeant rolled up. Getting out, he looked questioningly at the two officers standing outside their car with the obviously drunk man in the back seat.

"What's going on, fellas?" Both deputies quickly filled him in on what had transpired, and asked what they should do next.

The sergeant rolled his eyes. "If that's what he wants, just take the guy to jail. You can look at him and see he's drunk." But as the three cops turned around, they were surprised to see the man standing outside the patrol car.

"Hey, you," ordered the sergeant. "Get back in there."

"No," said the man with a belch.

"Look," said the sergeant more sternly, "I said get back in the car."

"But I don't want to go to jail now," the man drawled.

"But you said you were drunk!" cried the first deputy.

"Well, I changed my mind," declared the man, swaying on his feet. "I don't drunk…I'm as think as…I thought, I mean…"

"Yeah, right," the sergeant said. "But you're going to jail, and that's it. Now get back in the car." But as he placed his hand on the man's arm, the drunk tore away and tried to resist. In a half-second, all three deputies were struggling to control the large man.

"Couldn't get him out," grunted the first deputy, "can't get him back in."

After a few minutes of straining, swearing, and pushing, the deputies were finally able to handcuff the drunk and secure him in the back seat of the cop car.

"Take that moron to jail," huffed the sergeant as he stomped off to his car. "I'm going to get me something to drink."

The two young deputies got back into their police car and drove out of the truck stop parking lot. Behind them, the man swayed back and forth with a large grin on his face.

"Can we stop somewhere on the way?" he asked. "I'm kinda hungry."

"No!" yelled both of the cops in unison as they turned onto the highway and headed for the jail.

Pray Without Ceasing

Throughout the midnight shift, the male deputy and his female partner had gone about their patrol duties with only a few incidents. As the shift waned into the early morning hours, they had started checking the churches in their patrol area. Each officer would take turns getting out, checking the church doors, and leaving a small tag that would show the congregation members that the building had been checked during the night.

On a dark stretch of road, the patrol car pulled slowly up to a brick church building.

"Your turn," said the male officer, tossing the packet of tags to his partner.

"I got it," she said. An experienced officer herself, the female deputy got out of the car as she had done numerous times during the night. The beam from her flashlight illuminated the front of the church, and she saw nothing amiss. Stopping at the door, she tore a new tag from her packet and reached down to check the door. A chill ran up her spine when the doorknob turned in her hand.

Her training kicking in, she stepped to the side of her unlocked door and flashed her light at her partner. Knowing immediately what she had found, he slid out of the patrol car and joined the female officer beside the door.

"Unlocked?" he whispered. His partner nodded. Drawing their weapons, they gently opened the door and stepped into the dark church.

The beams of their flashlights danced across the floor and walls as the two deputies checked for any intruders who might have entered the building. A church is a creepy place at night, an almost surreal, crypt-like place. The officers separated, each taking an individual aisle in order to better cover the sanctuary. The only sound was their boots pressing the soft carpet, and their quietly nervous breathing.

The female officer moved along very slowly, checking each row of pews. She saw nothing but carefully placed songbooks and bibles in the wooden racks. Her partner had gotten to the front of the room before she had, and her heartbeat quickened when she saw him stop suddenly and point his weapon at something in front of him as he motioned her to where he stood.

Grasping her weapon even tighter, she stepped quickly to her partner's side. Her light showed her what he was seeing: two legs stretched out on the floor beside the front pew. Then, she caught her breath. Not one, but two forms lay face down on the carpet. Two men, dressed in blue jeans and T-shirts. Their hands lay hidden underneath them.

The deputies took their positions, leveling their weapons at the two bodies. The female officer quickly radioed to the dispatcher what they had found. As she replaced the radio on her belt, her partner shouted with a loud voice:

"*Sheriff's department! Show us your hands!*"

The two bodies jerked at the order, and seemed to slowly come to life. With wide eyes, the two men rolled over and shielded their eyes from the bright flashlights.

"Don't move!" ordered the female officer. "Keep your hands where we can see them!"

"Now, wait just a minute," said one of the men with a trembling voice. "You don't understand..."

"All we want to know," said the male officer, "is who you are and what you're doing in here."

"Nothing!" pleaded the other man, obviously unnerved. "We were just praying!"

"What?" asked both officers together.

"The preacher knows," said the first man, "We wanted to pray all night. And he gave us permission to use the church."

"Do you have any idea what time it is?" asked the male deputy. "It's after two in the morning!"

"Oh," said the man, somewhat embarrassed, "I guess we must have fallen asleep."

Obtaining the men's identification, the female officer had the dispatcher call the preacher. Sure enough, he sleepily confirmed the men's story.

"You guys should at least leave a light on," said the male officer as he gave them back their IDs. "I'm sure you see how this looked to us when we found the door unsecured."

"I suppose it looked pretty suspicious," said one of the men. "But we want you to know how much we appreciate how you keep an eye on our building at night."

The officers reholstered their weapons and left the building, shaking their heads as their adrenaline levels subsided.

"All my life I've heard, 'Pray without ceasing,' joked the male deputy to his partner. "But this is the first time I've seen it taken literally."

Before the night was over, both deputies had said a few silent prayers themselves.

First Day for the Rookie

There are few other levels of bravado that can compare with the police officer fresh out of the police academy. After eight to ten weeks of learning to walk like a cop, talk like a cop, and shoot like a cop, you've learned to do all of the cop-like things that the police do, like drive those shiny and fast police cars. Isn't that every little boy's dream?

So it's no surprise for the rookie officer to report to work that first day after his academy graduation with the feeling that he should have a big "S" on his chest and a red cape on his back. He is now a super hero, able to leap tall buildings and catch criminals by the handfuls. Or at least that's what he feels like.

And so it was one sunny day when a new deputy reported for work, eager to begin his career in law enforcement. After a brief orientation and meeting with his Sheriff, he was assigned a shiny new police car, complete with lights and sirens. Even before he pulled out of the parking lot, he was raring to go.

And even before he pulled out of the jail parking lot, he saw the van speed down the highway. Speeding! Of all the dastardly deeds! Not in his county! So the new deputy pulled off in pursuit of his first catch, the first criminal prey of his career. As he gained on the suspect vehicle, he turned on his lights and siren to signal the offender to pull over. But the van only slowed a little, and continued to drive away. The deputy's heart leapt with excitement. It was just like all of the videos he had watched at the academy! He was in a real, honest-to-goodness car chase! On his first day!

He radioed the situation to his dispatcher and requested other officers to come to his assistance. He knew the excitement in his voice betrayed his inexperience, but to catch this fleeing suspect would prove his skills to his fellow officers. The van turned onto a side road, and he doggedly followed, lights and siren blaring.

Other deputies arrived, closing in on the van and the new officer. The van made another turn, and only came to a stop when the road was blocked by another squad car. The new deputy leapt from his car, eager to face the first criminal he had snatched. As he stepped boldly to the door of the van, the other officers gathered around. And for a moment, the new deputy didn't quite know what to say.

The driver of the van was an elderly woman, obviously surprised at being stopped by the police. When the new deputy finally regained his composure and spoke to the woman, he found that not only was she elderly, but she was also hard of hearing. It seemed that the reason she had not stopped for his siren was simply because she could not hear it. As his fellow officers giggled quietly among themselves, the new deputy would not be deterred. After all, the woman had broken the law, and she was going to get a ticket for her reckless speed. He confidently wrote out the citation, trying his best to salvage his dignity in front of the veteran officers who had come to back him up. But when he had given the elderly driver her copy of the ticket, her response was priceless. It took every ounce of self-control for the veteran cops to get back to their own cars before they burst out laughing.

As he handed the woman the ticket, she simply smiled and said, "Oh, this isn't so bad. I'm sure I can get this taken care of."

"Oh?" said the cocky new rookie. "And just how do you think you'll do that?"

"Because," answered the lady sweetly, "I'm the Sheriff's grandmother."

A Star Asleep in the Dark

The deputy was new to the department, a likeable guy, good-looking, and an ex-college athlete. He caught on fast in his patrol duties and had done well in the police academy. His supervisors found him to be polite, intelligent, and hard working, and they saw he was going to make a good cop. Like most new officers, he was placed on the midnight shift.

Therein, he developed his only problem.

Although he was one of the best cops on the beat, the late hours were hard on him. Around 2:00 or 3:00 A.M. every night, he became uncontrollably sleepy. So sleepy, in fact, that he worried that he might fall asleep and crash his patrol car. So, to hide his affliction, he found several out-of-the-way places and would regularly hide and sneak out a nap in order to make it through the night shift.

For a while, he kept up the ruse very well. When the calls quieted down, he would slip away to one of his hiding places, park his car, lean back in the driver's seat, and go to sleep. To make sure he didn't sleep through any calls, he simply turned his radio volume up high enough to hear his unit number, "One-thirty-one," which would wake him if he were needed. Several months passed by, and his late-night napping remained undetected. He became so comfortable with the situation that he began to sleep more and more soundly.

But one night, a fellow officer saw the patrol car parked away in a dark location and became concerned over the welfare of his fellow officer. Upon investigation, he found the rookie sound asleep in the driver's seat. The officer considered what he should do in this strange situation, so he left the rookie asleep and called for their shift supervisor.

The veteran sergeant rolled up minutes later and was quietly taken over to the rookie's car. Still, the new cop slept like a baby. The sergeant wrinkled his nose at the rookie's dozing form and walked back to his patrol car.

"What are you going to do, Sarge?" asked the other officer. "He's a good cop, and I don't want to get him into any trouble. But he could get himself killed like this."

The Sergeant thought silently for a moment, then used his cell phone to instruct the dispatcher to page all other deputies on the shift, and have them meet him at the location of their sleeping coworker. Then, from his trunk, he removed a large piece of dark canvas he kept with him for emergency situations.

"I think we'd better nip this in the bud," the veteran sergeant said to the other deputy. "We'll teach him a lesson he won't forget."

When the rest of the deputies on the shift arrived, the sergeant took them aside and explained his plan. The other men hid their giggles as best as they could while they assisted the sergeant in spreading the large piece of dark canvas over the sleeping rookie's patrol car, being very careful not to wake him. The canvas was dark enough to keep out any light, and completely covered the windows and doors of the rookie's car. Then, stepping back to get a full view of the festivities, the other officers watched as the sergeant turned on his portable radio and very urgently said, "One-thirty-one!"

The rookie's patrol car suddenly shook violently. Then the engine turned on and revved up several times, but the car just sat still.

"One-thirty-one!" repeated the sergeant into his radio.

Then the rookie's headlights came on, and the deputies heard more shaking inside the car, then the sound of the gearshift moving back and forth. They shook with held-in laughter, some kneeling on the ground, unable to stand.

"One-thirty-one!" the sergeant yelled into the radio the third time.

Suddenly, the door of the rookie's car burst open, and the young man spilled out on to the ground, wide-eyed with terror. The sight of their new partner with such an incredulous look on his face was too much for the other deputies. The entire group began horse-laughing, slapping their knees and falling to the ground. The rookie sheepishly regained his feet, realizing he'd been had.

"You know, that's a good way to get killed out here," said the sergeant with a grin as he crossed his arms over his broad chest. "We thought we would help you remember how someone could walk up to your patrol car and shoot you while you're in there taking a nap."

But the other cops only laughed harder when the young deputy leaned shakily against his car and said, "All I know is, there for a minute I thought I'd gone blind."

He never again felt like taking a nap on duty.

Just Doing Their Part

The State Trooper who supervised the litter prevention program was a large, handsome, muscular black sergeant whose imposing appearance hid a jovial, tenderhearted man with a good sense of humor. His record of convictions for illegal dumping was well known around the state, as well as within his district.

One of the reasons the sergeant had such a high success rate was the fact that he wasted no time in his investigations. Once he received information about an illegal dumpsite, he began working it immediately, looking for clues as to who had unlawfully disposed of garbage. Often, people left envelopes with addresses and other personal effects in their trash, so it was fairly simple to establish a few leads.

When he heard about the dumpsite on Pond Road, he characteristically went straight to the scene. Sure enough, a large area near the old rural pond was covered in garbage, old tires, a few mattresses, and other pieces of debris. The big man waded out into the middle of the junk, poking through the refuse as he carefully searched for clues. He was particularly incensed at the Pond Road site, as it had been a fairly pleasant place before the litterers had ruined it.

After collecting several envelopes and papers that bore some suspected addresses, the trooper returned to his patrol car and drove to the top of the hill near the main road. He stopped at this high spot that overlooked the old pond and wrote a quick report of his preliminary investigation. Finishing up, he noticed a pickup truck driving down Pond Road far below him. The truck's bed appeared full of trash. Curious, he waited and watched.

Sure enough, the pickup truck backed up to the dumpsite by the water, and two men got out. Using shovels, the two litterers began unloading the trash from the truck to the ground. The big trooper grinned and waited until the two had over half of their truck unloaded before he pulled his patrol car down the hill and up to the dumpsite.

As he came closer, he noticed something that gave him a good laugh. When the two men saw the patrol car, they immediately stopped shoveling refuse from the truck into the dumpsite and began shoveling from the dumpsite back into the truck.

"What's going on?" asked the big officer with a friendly smile as he exited his patrol unit.

"Oh, not much officer," answered one of the men as he wiped sweat from his brow. "Just cleaning up this here dump."

"Well, well," said the officer, "that's a commendable thing to be doing. I really appreciate you helping me out like that."

"Just doin' our part, Sir," lied the man with an innocent look.

"I'm sure you are," grinned the big trooper. Leaning casually on the side of the truck, the officer took his time, making small talk with the two men as they labored under the hot sun to reload every piece of garbage they had thrown out. The trooper made sure they loaded quite a bit extra, too, just for good measure.

But the friendly conversation became sour as the trooper wrote each of the men a citation for illegal dumping. It was no coincidence that their names matched a few of the letters that the trooper had picked up. He was also careful to follow the men as they drove to the county landfill, paid the fee, and disposed of their trash in a lawful manner.

When the case went to court, the men quietly paid their fines and offered no defense to the trooper's charges.

Blind and Deaf to a Hundred Dollar Bill

"You wanna do something fun?"

The detective rubbed the sleep from his eyes as he tried to wake up to the phone call that had roused him from his evening nap.

"What are you talking about?"

The detective on the other end of the line laughed malevolently. "Get down to the station. We've got an undercover drug buy to make on Alice Brown. I want you to be the narc."

"No way," said the sleepy young detective. "She's seen me before. She knows who I am."

"She'll buy," reasoned the other detective. "She won't be looking at your handsome face, just at that money in your hand."

"Oh, man," groaned the sleepy officer. It was almost 11:30 at night.

"Just get down here," ordered his partner. "It'll be fun."

It was midnight by the time the officers met at the station, and almost 1:00 A.M. before the briefing and planning were completed. At 1:30 A.M., the young detective approached the residence, which was in a low-income housing complex. In another car outside, four other officers waited, listening in on the wire the young detective wore under his army surplus jacket.

Alice answered the door and saw a younger man in an army coat with a cap pulled down over his eyes. From his pocket, he drew out a hundred dollar bill, and Alice's eyes flashed. She knew the routine, so with a quick look around outside, she waved him in.

The narc had been in Alice's apartment before, and it had changed very little. Dirty clothes littered the floor, along with assorted trash and leftover food. Still, she seemed not to recognize him. He pretended to be nervous, shrugging his shoulders and not speaking. He simply held up five fingers, a sign that Alice knew well.

"Ain't got five bags," Alice said, shaking her head. "Only got four left. Just four."

The narc waived her away, and held up five fingers again, shaking his hand in her face.

"I said I ain't got no five!" Swore Alice. "You take what I got or nothin' at all!"

The narc dropped his hand and shrugged. Alice snorted, and turned to walk into her kitchen. It was then the narc saw Alice's father.

The elderly man had been in trouble most of his life. Hard living had taken its toll on him, though, and a stroke a few years back had left him in a wheel chair and unable to speak. But when he rolled into the living room, his eyes widened as he immediately recognized the detective. As Alice passed by, her father began waiving his hands and pointing. The detective, thinking the jig was up, prepared to reach for his weapon.

But Alice still had the hundred-dollar bill on her mind. "Oh shut up, you ole' fool. What you actin' so crazy 'bout?" The old man continued to point angrily at the narc in his living room. "You just hush, or I'll lock you back in the bedroom," said Alice as she removed four large bags of marijuana from her stash in the kitchen. As she passed by him again, the old man beat the handles of his wheelchair with his fists, furious. "I told you to shut up, fool." Cursed Alice, ignoring him. She walked back to face the narc and exchanged the bags for the hundred dollar bill.

As she eyed the greenback, the narc whispered, "There's just one more thing: You're under arrest." As he spoke, he snapped a handcuff on one of Alice's wrists. Her eyes widened as she realized she'd been had. With no other recourse, she tried to hand the hundred dollar bill back to the detective.

"I don't think so," he said as the other four officers entered the door.

"Oh, come on now," she pleaded, "Please don't take me to jail. Come on now, please? I ain't done much. Come on, now."

"Sit on the couch, Alice," said the young detective. "We've got a warrant to search the place."

For the next several minutes, Alice continued to beg for a break while the officers looked for more dope. Nothing else was found, and the detectives noticed that Alice had grown quiet. Walking back to the living room, they found her still on the couch, smoking her last joint. The big detective snatched it out of her mouth, crushed it out, and placed it in an evidence bag.

"Why you gotta be that way?" cried Alice as the detective's lifted her to her feet. She turned to her elderly father in his wheelchair. "Why didn't you tell me he was a cop, you useless ole' fool?"

Her father glared at her, furious at both his inability to speak and his inability to walk across the room and strangle her. He simply looked at her straight in the eye, stuck out his tongue, and raised his middle finger.

Churches, Snakes, and Bats! Oh, My!

Cops are supposed to be fearless and tough. That's what society expects: men and women who can handle any situation calmly and with enough guts to take on all the criminals in the world. A badge and a gun make a cop something of a superhero, able to run faster than a fleeing suspect, and to leap tall felons with a single bound.

And so it may come as a surprise to some that cops, like a lot of people, have things they are very much afraid of. And it's not the thug with a gun, or the murderer, or the three hundred pound convict ready to fight. Cops are afraid of other stuff.

Like church buildings at night.

It may sound silly, but it's true. There are few places around that are more dark and spooky than a church building at night. Especially those in rural areas with no other houses around. It is a cop's job to get out of the nice, safe patrol car, walk through the churchyard, past the cemetery with the gray gravestones that rise ominously in the moonlight, up to the church to perform his nightly patrol. And worse yet, when the officer checks the door and finds it unlocked, a cold chill runs up his spine when he knows it is his duty to go inside the dark building in order to make sure no criminal activity is afoot. This has often caused problems, especially when the preacher has decided to work late at night. Let me tell you: guns, preachers, dark churches, and scared cops don't mix well. Not at all.

And then there are bats. I have a good friend, a state trooper actually, who is terrified of bats. He is convinced that the little animals are spawns of the devil and will lay eggs in his hair and drive him crazy. It is a mighty lucky speeder who gets stopped at night by this trooper, when a bat begins to flitter around overhead. The trooper gets a wild look in his eyes as he watches the tiny wings flap above him. He might let the driver go with a warning, rather than have the horrible creature circling in the night sky, just waiting to sink his little vampire teeth in the troopers neck. He'd have bad dreams for weeks.

Of course, snakes are high on the list as well. Police officers go on a lot of wild animal calls, and some involve long, slithering reptiles. I once knew of a fireman who responded to a snake call along with a snake-hating cop. The fireman calmly picked up the overly large snake, and knowing the officer's phobia, turned as if to throw the snake on him. You can imagine the fireman's surprise when he found himself looking down the barrel of a large caliber handgun, the officer growling with a shaky voice, "If you throw that thing on me I swear to heaven I'll kill you." He wasn't kidding.

Police officers don't have the market cornered on fear and anxiety. An EMT I once knew could handle anything: the blood, the gore, the accident scenes. He could do it all. But when it came time to performing CPR on a patient, something didn't jive. During the procedure, he would inevitably become violently sick, even to the point of vomiting into the side door compartment of the ambulance as it raced to the hospital. Another EMT, very skilled and experienced, would suffer an attack of anxiety, during the ride to a serious call, so severe that it required his partner to stop the ambulance at the first restroom they could find, sometimes several times, on the way. Once at the scene, he would become calm and competent.

We forget sometimes that cops and other emergency personnel are people, too. We all have something we're afraid of, or something that terrifies us to the point of a nervous breakdown. As for myself, I'll just say this:

You'd better keep that spider away from me. Remember, I have a gun.

That's Not Mine, Either

The officer was running radar when the big Lincoln sped by, well above the legal speed limit. Pulling the patrol car off in pursuit, it took quite a bit of effort for the officer to catch up to the Lincoln, but the driver pulled over to the tune of the officer's blue lights and siren.

The officer stepped up to the driver's door, where a young man in his twenties sat looking pleasantly at the cop. He'd already taken out his driver's license and handed it out the window before even being asked to do so.

"Good morning, Officer." Said the young man cordially.

"Good morning, Sir," said the officer. He examined the license, then looked back to the young man. "Mr. Thomas, do you know why I stopped you?"

"No, Sir," said the young man in a singsong voice.

"You were doing 80 in a 45 zone," answered the officer. "Can I see the registration on your vehicle?"

"This car?" asked the young man. "This car's not mine. I just borrowed it from a friend. I'm not sure where he keeps his "

"I see," said the officer. "I've already run the plates, so we'll see what comes back on it." The officer noticed a sudden odor; a sweet, smoky smell that was a characteristic of freshly burned marijuana. Looking inside the vehicle, he noticed a ball cap lying on a plastic bag in the front seat. The bag was full of a green leafy substance.

"What's that on the seat beside you?"

The young man glanced over at the bag, then back at the officer. With innocent eyes, he shrugged. "Gee, Officer, I don't know what that is."

"I see," said the officer. "Perhaps you should step out of the vehicle."

The driver got out of the vehicle, still very cordial and accommodating. The officer reached in and took out the bag, opened it and smelled of the contents.

"Is this your marijuana?" asked the cop.

The young man looked startled. "Is that what that is? I hadn't even noticed it."

"Is this yours?" the officer asked again.

"Oh, no," said the young man, as if he were pure as the driven snow, "That's not mine."

The officer's dispatcher called and informed him that the vehicle's tags were expired. When he told the young man he could be charged with violating registration laws, the man kept a straight and concerned face as he replied the same, "Like I said, this car isn't mine."

Beginning to get the picture of what he was dealing with, the officer called for a wrecker. Then he asked the man to place his hands on the car for a pat-down. Sure enough, a large bulge in the young man's front pocket proved to be yet another bag of pot, and included some rolling papers and a half-smoked joint.

Holding the bag of drugs up to the young man, the officer tried to keep a straight face himself as he asked, "Can you explain this?"

The young man sucked in his breath. "Oh, that's not mine either."

The officer couldn't resist a gasp. "Not yours? I took this right out of your pocket! How could it not be yours? It was in your pants, for crying out loud!"

"Oh, these pants," said the young man. "These pants aren't mine either."

"What?"

"Yeah, these pants aren't mine. I spent the night at a buddy's house last night after a big party. I guess I must have picked up somebody else's pants and put them on." The man never flinched as he looked the officer straight in the eye.

Having heard it all, the officer just shook his head. "You're under arrest for reckless driving, violation of registration, and possession of narcotics and paraphernalia. Those charges are all yours." He took out his handcuffs and snapped them on the young man's wrists. "See these? These are yours, too." He then led the youth back to the patrol car, opened the door, and assisted the man into the back seat. "See this?" asked the officer with a grin, "This is your seat. The charges, the handcuffs, and this ride to jail. They're all yours. It sounds like you don't have anything, but now you can say you definitely have something."

No longer able to keep up his lies, the driver slumped his shoulders and pouted. "Whatever," he said as the officer closed the door.

Tears of a Clown

The highway patrolman yawned as he stared at the highway in front of him. It was late, well after midnight, and the officer was tired. Taillights appeared in the distance in front of him, and the Trooper noticed it was a van. As he watched, his senses and attention came awake again as the van continuously drifted over the centerline, and by all appearances the driver looked to be intoxicated. The Trooper turned on his blue lights and followed the van as it pulled to the side of the highway. He approached the driver and was quite surprised at what he saw.

The driver was dressed like a clown.

It seemed the gentleman was the owner of a clown-rental business and was returning from a late-night party where he'd made an appearance. He still had on the suit with the polka-dots, the crazy wig, and make-up complete with a red nose. He was also under the influence of what was found out later to be a large amount of prescription medication. For all practical purposes the Trooper had pulled over a drunken clown.

Trying to maintain an air of professionalism, the Trooper asked the man to exit his vehicle and after a brief talk, directed the painted man through a series of field sobriety tests. Big shoes and all, the clown performed the tests poorly due to his inebriated state and even had quite a bit of difficulty in placing his index finger on his big red nose.

It must have been quite a sight for the people passing by that night to see a clown standing in front of a blue-lighted highway patrol car, trying to walk a straight line.

Convinced the clown was driving under the influence, the Trooper informed the man he was under arrest, and directed him to place his hands on the front of the patrol car in order to be handcuffed. It was at this point that the clown became angry, and despite the made-up smile on his face, he refused to cooperate with the Trooper. When the officer took the clown by his arm, the fight was on.

Once again, we can only imagine the impression left on passing motorists as they drove by. It's not just any night you see a clown fighting a highway patrolman on the side of the road. People must have been thinking, *Did I really see what I think I did?*

Lucky for the officer, the clown was not armed with a seltzer bottle.

Finally, with his big, red-haired wig pushed to the side and his make-up smeared, the clown was subdued and placed in the back seat of the patrol car. A wrecker was called to tow the van, and the wrecker driver almost fell over laughing at the sight of Bozo in the back of the patrol car.

The clown, forlorn and angry under his greasepaint smile, just shook his head and said, "This ain't a bit funny."

Alcohol, Tractors, and Trailers

Only in the South could it happen. Only in a rural East Tennessee County could such a dastardly deed be done. Nowhere else could a disgruntled defendant drink too much alcohol, take on county deputies with a gun and a tractor, and the whole thing over a house trailer.

Such was the case in Meigs County, Tennessee, this week. It seems a Meigs County resident was suspected of leasing a mobile home where an illegal methamphetamine lab had been operating, and had been ordered by the court to vacate the property within ten days. The defendant did not comply, or at least not according to the reports filed by local officials. It seems the gentleman was angry, got drunk, armed himself, and decided to destroy his mobile home. His choice of a weapon of mass destruction was a farm tractor. Maybe there should be a background check and a cooling off period before someone gets handed the keys to a weapon like a farm tractor, but I digress. Not only did he (allegedly) destroy some mobile homes, but he also rammed the tractor into several parked vehicles. When deputies arrived, the man, evidently emboldened by the alcohol in his brain and the horsepower under his seat, brandished a firearm and refused to surrender. Then, revving up the tractor, he rammed the patrol car, and attempted to escape. The officers followed him, in what I would assume to be a not-so-high-speed chase, and once again confronted him at a local business. For a second time, the gentleman refused to surrender, and again tried to ram the officers with the tractor. So the deputies, realizing the imminent danger, immediately took steps to halt any further aggression. Relying on their training, they fired their guns. And shot out one of the tractor tires. The defendant, realizing the deputies meant business and seeing his getaway vehicle disabled, did the smart thing and surrendered.

I truly love this part of the country, and when an incident like this happens, I remember just why I love it. Things like this just don't happen anywhere else. Criminals in New York City or Chicago would never even consider using a farm tractor to commit a crime, much less as a getaway car. And to think it could happen, in of all places, a trailer park. Why, this story has all the ingredients of an appearance on *Jerry Springer*.

Of course, the newspaper reports quoted the sheriff as saying that "alcohol was probably involved." Certainly sounds like it was. The element of proof will lie in a court of law, but I would hope that a judge or jury would take for granted that a sober person would have picked something else to drive besides a tractor.

What makes me wonder is the thought pattern behind this criminally masterminded scheme. Did he have a particular fondness for the destructive force of a front-end loader? Or was it the lure of power over speed? And just what is it this guy has against mobile homes?

While it is easy to see the humor in this story, one can realize just how easily a life could have been lost, whether it was one of the officers, the defendant, or a bystander. It is truly a miracle that no one was killed, and credit is due the officers, who, in the words of Sheriff Walter Hickman, "handled the situation very well and were able to bring the matter under control without any unnecessary injuries being received by any of the parties involved." While we can laugh now, it may be a while before the officers involved see any humor in the situation whatsoever.

But I think one day in the not too distant future, they will. It's not an everyday you can catch a criminal whose tools of the trade are a trailer, a tractor, a gun, a beer, and a bad attitude

This Stuff Really Happens

Some things you just can't make up. Strange things happen, and as they say, "the truth is stranger than fiction." Below are several examples of the strange and the humorous that police officers see and experience every day.

After a shakedown at the jail, an overweight inmate who tended to hoard food in his cell sent the following letter to the jail administrator:

I want you to know that during the recent shakedown, some of the officers were eating out of the jail commissary, which belongs to us prisoners, not the officers. I would also like to report a Theft Under $500, because I am missing the following two items from my cell: a Snickers Bar and a Moon Pie. I will press charges when I find out who took them.

Two inmates who broke out of jail during the winter months seemed to have put very little thought into planning their escape. The overnight temperature had been below freezing, and according to the arresting officer's report, the two escapees were easily apprehended the next day due to the fact that they were both suffering from exposure. It seems that in their haste to leave the warmth of their cells, the two men had worn only T-shirts and underwear during the course of their escape.

While taking a theft report, an officer asked the complainant how he was sure that he was missing $500. The officer was surprised when the man candidly said, "I only have $200 on me. I know that $500 was stolen because I had made $700 from selling methamphetamine."

While opening court one morning, the court officer said the usual "Hear ye, hear ye" followed by instructions for anyone having cell phones, pagers, or any other electronic device to please turn them off. When the officer finished, a little voice from an elderly woman in the back of the courtroom said, "Does that include pacemakers?"

A district attorney was cross-examining an elderly defendant charged in a motor vehicle accident.

"Mr. Vincent, will you tell the court if you wear prescription glasses?"

"I do," said the man.

"And Mr. Vincent, will you tell the court if you had your glasses on at the time of the accident?"

"No, Sir, I didn't have them on."

The DA then broke the cardinal rule of cross examination: knowing when to stop.

"Mr. Vincent, will you tell the court just how far you can see without your glasses?"

"Well," replied the sharp old man, "I can see the moon. How far do you reckon that is?"

A judge called out the name of a defendant charged with public drunkenness. As the old codger shuffled down the courtroom aisle, the Judge continued in a sing-song voice, "Mr. Newman...Mr. Newman, you are charged with public drunkenness. What shall we do with you, Mr. Newman?"

"Not very much, judge," the drunk drawled as he shuffled to the bench, "Not very much."

After obtaining a search warrant to enter the home of a suspected drug dealer, officers carefully planned and executed the entry of the residence. After the arrest, officers reported that when they went through the door, they discovered the suspected drug dealer "sitting on the couch, smoking a joint and watching an episode of COPS."

Officers approached a man and advised him that there was an outstanding arrest warrant for him on a charge of writing bad checks. In an effort to avoid incarceration, the suspect asked if there was any way he could simply pay off the amount of the bad checks. The officers refused the man and placed him under arrest after he had produced a checkbook and offered to write them a check for the delinquent amount.

Officers can go through a tremendous amount of stress on the job. Sometimes the stress can eat into an officer's attention span. For example, a state trooper I know was going to lunch during an extremely busy shift. On his way, he decided to get some gas and stop by an ATM. The Trooper pulled up to the ATM, got out of his car, unscrewed the cap to his gas tank, and reached to the ATM for the gas nozzle. About that time, he glanced up at the bank's drive-in window and saw several bank employees watching him with expressions of *What in the heck are you doing?* The Trooper very calmly replaced his gas cap, got into his car, and drove away, too embarrassed to even get some cash from the ATM.

Part Two

Sometimes, even humor isn't enough. Cops, firefighters, and EMTs are all people underneath those uniforms. It's easy to forget that they bleed, cry, and have tender hearts just like everybody else.

One Tiny Little Hand

EMTs and Paramedics work strange hours and see things that would prevent a normal person from ever sleeping again. It is a demanding job that can go from routine to nightmare in a matter of minutes. And while many calls can be gruesome tragedies, it is sometimes the little things that Medics see that stay with them for the rest of their lives.

For several days, the Paramedic knew what he was about to be asked to do. Unlike an emergency call that may come when he least expected it, this time he knew exactly where he would be going and who he would be caring for. During the days leading up to the transport, the Medic called the hospital several times to talk to doctors, social workers, and nurses to get all the information he could about the patient he would be caring for. He mulled over the impending call, thinking constantly about what he would be doing. Finally, the day arrived, and the Paramedic and his EMT partner went to the hospital to pick up their patient.

The baby had been born some twelve weeks premature. A little boy, he had been born to a single mother who had once been addicted to methamphetamine. Seeing the serious condition of her child, she decided to give him up for adoption. That is, if the baby lived. The chances of the little boy's survival were very slim, and the doctors and nurses in the pediatric intensive care unit prepared to watch yet another baby succumb to overwhelming odds.

But someone had forgotten to tell the little boy he was doomed.

A husband and wife in a distant state adopted the tiny baby, and his new mother traveled to the hospital to spend what time she could with him, which she knew might only be days or weeks at best. Problems developed with his health, as were expected for such a premature infant. But as each seemingly insurmountable obstacle came upon him, he survived. As each time the touch of death seemed to be right around the corner, he reached out his tiny hands and held on. As the doctors and nurses who cared for him watched in disbelief, he emerged at the end of each day just a little stronger. He soon became well known among the hospital staff. They called him "the living miracle." And now, five months old, he was well enough to go home.

The Paramedic looked over the child's medical history as he prepared his paperwork for the trip. The baby had a list of health problems longer than most ninety-year-old nursing home patients he'd seen. But the medic was immediately impressed with the little life that stared up at him from the tangle of monitor cables and oxygen lines. Although he was five months old, he looked to be only a day-old newborn. But outside of the tracheal tube that helped him breath, he looked strong, even healthy. The medic felt a little less worried as one of the little hands reached up and took his finger in a strong, tight grip.

The child and his new mother were taken down to the waiting ambulance, and as he was placed inside the nursing staff began to cry as they said goodbye to the little boy who they had come to feel so close to. It was the first time that the infant had ever been taken out of the hospital, and the medic watched as his eyes widened at his first sight of sunshine, and sky, and the outdoors. As he was safely secured to the ambulance cot, the tiny boy also became entranced with a colorful mobile that the Medic had hung from the inside of the ambulance. The little eyes watched with wonder the red, black, and white clowns that slowly circled above him to the jingle of lullabies. The ambulance left the tear-filled hospital staff, and followed by the baby's new parents, began the eight-hour drive to his new home.

The Paramedic hovered over the little boy, constantly checking the readouts on the various monitors and oxygen lines. He watched carefully for any change in the child's condition, for even though he had overcome so much, the child was still considered to be a high risk infant on a critical transport. But although the Paramedic meticulously performed the work he was trained to do, there was something very different about his little patient.

Sometimes, the child would wrinkle his forehead, as a normal baby does when he is about to cry. But the little boy could make no sound due to the tracheal tube. The Medic, sensing his frustration, gently touched and petted his soft arms and legs and spoke very softly to the baby. The tiny hand would reach and grab the Medic's finger, and he would go to sleep, drifting off to the sounds of lullabies over the hum of the highway beneath them. The Paramedic was struck at the little round head covered in strawberry blonde hair. How healthy he looked, how strong he must be. Having no children of his own, the Medic felt something he'd never felt before, an overwhelming concern for a little life so helpless, yet so full of fight.

Finally, they arrived at their destination and the Paramedic and EMT took the little boy into his new home. They disconnected their monitors and placed the infant into his mother's arms. Suddenly, the Paramedic felt as if he could not leave. He stared at the child he'd cared for, and realized why the nursing staff at the hospital had been so emotional. He leaned over and kissed the soft face goodbye. Even though the family pleaded with them to stay for dinner before they returned home, they politely refused. The Paramedic knew that it was time for his parents to be with him. It was time to let him go.

Driving home through the night, the Paramedic silently recalled the many things he'd seen over the years. Sometimes he had come home disheartened over the times he'd seen death and loss. Sometimes he'd felt there was no purpose in what he did, but not tonight.

It was an ambulance call the paramedic would never forget.

Pretending to Be a Monster

The officer had been dispatched to the local Emergency Room, and he was uneasy. The dispatcher had given very little information, except to meet with the ER staff, and so the officer could only imagine what might be awaiting him. As he arrived, a nurse he knew met him at the door.

"What's going on?"

"Well," she began, "there's a fifteen-month-old baby in one of the rooms. His father brought him in saying he had the flu, but, well, you'd better come take a look at this."

He followed the nurse to one of the exam rooms where a young man dressed in an old T-shirt and blue jean shorts stood beside an older, overweight woman. Both were looking down at the small form lying on the exam bed in front of them. The baby, weak and malnourished, looked to be less than a year old, although he was at fifteen months. But what immediately caught the attention of the officer were the burns all over the baby's chest, back, and legs. Numerous and small, they were no bigger than the eraser of a pencil. He recognized them as the kind made by a cigarette.

"So," he said, pretending for a moment he had not seen the signs of abuse, "it looks like we've got a sick baby here."

"Yeah," answered the young man, "it's the flu." The woman only smiled weakly.

"That's too bad," said the officer, "it's sad to see a little one sick like that." He backed out of the room and motioned for the nurse to step over.

"That's a pretty bad case of the flu," he whispered sarcastically. "What did they say caused all of those burns?"

"We asked them, but they seemed not to know anything at all," said the nurse, rolling her eyes. "The doctor has given the baby some antibiotics, but didn't want to release them until you guys had a look."

The officer stepped back inside and made small talk with the man and woman until the release papers were signed, then he asked if the people would bring the baby to the station. The young man, who was the child's father, shrugged indifferently and said he guessed they could.

The officer noted that neither the man nor the woman asked why they had to go.

At the station, the officer asked some general questions to both the man and the woman, whom he found to be the young man's stepmother. When he was told by the woman that the baby might have been burned while on a camping trip in a nearby county, the officer placed a call to social services.

"There's not much we can do, since it was in another county," said the caseworker over the phone. "Unless you can get a confession. If you don't, just find out what you can, and we'll pass it on to law enforcement and social services in that county. That's about all we can do."

Frustrated, although he was careful not to show it, he then took the father into a back office. He administered a Miranda warning and began to ask specific questions about the burns on the baby's body.

"Oh, those have been on him for a while," said the father.

"How do you think they got there?"

"I dunno," he said, "I think I noticed them after we were camping with some friends. The baby had slept with my mother in the tent next to mine, and it was after that when I noticed the sores."

"OK," said the officer cheerfully, suppressing his anger and disgust for the moment. "And you didn't hear anything all night? You didn't hear the baby cry out?"

"Nope."

The officer wrote notes down on his report as the man spoke. He very carefully composed himself for what he was about to do. The words he was about to say would sicken him, but he had to pretend. He had to forget about the little boys he had of his own. For the next few minutes, he was going to have to get down on the level of the man in front of him. A low, low level, indeed.

"You want a cigarette?" asked the officer, producing a pack from his pocket.

"Sure." Said the man eagerly. "I need one."

"Yeah, you know, sometimes kids just get on your nerves, you know?"

"Sometimes," answered the man as he lit up.

The officer nodded. "It's easy to get tired of them, especially after you've worked all day, or you're trying to enjoy a camping trip, but they just won't behave."

"I guess so," shrugged the man.

"And so you have to get a little rough with them. You know, to make them mind. You gotta do what you gotta do, right? Sometimes I think about using a cigarette, you know, to teach them a lesson. You ever think about something like that?"

The man shifted his eyes nervously, and shrugged again. The officer talked more, but after a while, he saw that the man wasn't going to confess. The officer was tired of pretending to be the kind of man that would hurt a child. He began to grow angry, and decided to turn up the juice.

"So, the baby was right there in the tent right beside you, and you didn't hear a thing?"

"No, we just..."

"You mean you didn't hear the baby cry just once?" his voice began to take a sharpness to its tone. "You mean, when somebody was placing that hot, burning cigarette onto your baby's tender skin, you mean to tell me you didn't hear your little baby scream out? You expect me to believe that?"

The man avoided the officer's eyes, and took a long drag on the shrinking cigarette. "Look, man, I don't know how—"

"You don't know?" the officer hissed, slowly rising from the chair. He leaned over and grasped the sides of the table tightly. "Well, I think you do know how that kid got burned., and I think either you did it or you know who did it. But, you aren't man enough to say it."

The man tried to meet the officer's glare, but he could not. He just sat there, holding the cigarette with a barely trembling hand. A direct accusation, and he had given no reply. The officer knew in his heart of hearts that he was right.

But the man would say little and eventually began to refuse to answer at all. Realizing he might jeopardize the case for the other agencies, the officer backed off. With no charges, he called the neighboring county's sheriff's department who sent a car to pick up the man for further questioning. The officers reluctantly allowed the woman to leave with the baby. There was nothing else they could do.

But the officer knew he had gotten close. He had pushed back some of the layers of deception, and he hoped that the other agency could dig deeper to find the truth. Or at least enough of the truth to charge whomever had harmed a defenseless child.

Later that night, the officer dropped by his home and looked in on the sleeping little boys he loved. Standing there in the darkness, he wondered what kind of a monster could take a cigarette and...no, he could not even imagine it.

Quietly, he kissed them and walked back out into the night.

There Won't Always Be Happy Endings

A very good friend of mine asked me a question a few days ago. He had read a recent story I had written for this column, which dealt with a troubling case of child abuse. The story ended with the police officer turning the suspect over to another agency, although he knew the man was responsible for the abuse of his own baby.

"I know there must be a second part to that one," declared my friend. "Surely there's a second part, where the officer gets the guy."

As much as I hated to say it, I could only shake my head.

"No," I replied, "Not that time."

One of the most frustrating things that police officers have to deal with is knowing in their heart of hearts the truth that someone is guilty, all the while knowing that there is not enough evidence to make an arrest or to convict. The facts are just not there for a court to decide upon, but the truth is. Sometimes, facts and truth are not necessarily the same things.

Our great country is based upon freedoms and certain rights that each citizen has and enjoys. Whether a person is a pillar of the community or a cold-blooded murderer of innocent people, we all have the same rights. Police cannot beat a confession out of a suspect, even though they know that the person is guilty, and even though they sometimes want to. It's simply not right, and although our collective opinions may cause us to have a desire to see a person pay for what they have done, it's simply not right to take it upon ourselves to exact justice. To do so would make the officer, and even the citizen, become the kind of person they hate.

That is the part that is so often very hard for police officers. They have to put away their "human" emotions in order to be fair and decent. But when you face a man who has been putting out his cigarettes on his little baby's skin, it's oh, so hard. But you do what is right, and you do your job.

Firefighters and EMTs feel the same type of frustration, just in a different way. I have good friends who have been forced to watch people die because they were unable to get to them in time. Houses have burned down because there wasn't enough manpower or water at the scene. Paramedics have crawled inside wrecked cars and assisted in hour-long extrications, only to have the victim die in their arms. It's a wonderful thing to possess the advanced training that police, firefighters, and EMTs have. But there are times when those skills are not enough. And when you sit with your head in your hands thinking over and over if you could have done something different, you wonder if all of that training was for nothing.

Unlike television and movies, there is not always a happy ending. Sometimes, bad guys get away. Sometimes, the hero dies for no reason. And although we want to find the end, the closure, that will allow us to put a traumatic event behind us, we can't. That, too, is frustrating. And emergency workers know that tomorrow may only bring more of the same.

All you can do is look down deep inside yourself and know that you did everything you could. You know that you played by the rules. You held on to your integrity and to your humanity, and those are what separate you from the monsters you deal with.

It's often an empty victory. But sometimes, you've just got to take victories as you can get them.

The Darkness of an Early Morning

The cool morning air was suddenly filled with a flurry of red and blue flashing lights, as a report came from the interstate that an accident had occurred. Police officers, EMTs, and Rescue personnel fought tired and sleepy eyes as they rushed to the scene.

Cars were backed up for several miles as some motorists had stopped to render what aid they could before the arrival of the emergency services. As police cars, fire trucks, and ambulances arrived, they saw a debris trail scattered all across the roadway and off both sides of the shoulder. A female victim lay on the roadside, covered in a white sheet by one of the motorists. Officers and EMTs glanced under the sheet, and saw immediately the foul death beneath. Some of the rescue workers, knowing there was nothing else they could do, gathered around the still form and quietly bowed their heads in prayer.

On the other side of the road, a vehicle sat on its top. No other victims were inside, but rescue workers found an empty child restraint seat that had been tossed out onto the grass. For several minutes, the responders searched anxiously over the scene, hoping and praying they would not find that a child had been involved in the wreck as well. But no other victim could be found, and the workers all whispered still more prayers of thankfulness. Most had seen tragedy before, and none wished to see anymore than they had to.

A state trooper arrived. He had been on his way home, but he now found himself finishing off his midnight shift by working a fatality. His trained eye saw the flecks of paint on the guardrail, the skid marks in the grass and across the highway to where the vehicle had flipped over numerous times before coming to rest. The forces exerted on the occupant must have been tremendous, judging from the condition of the body and its distance from the skid marks.

Another indication of the severity of the impact was the discovery of a wig that had been thrown out of the vehicle and had landed some 100 feet away. The state trooper made some jokes about the wig, and some of the other officers laughed. But it was gallows humor, and the jokes and laughter were only to relieve some of the stress of being at the scene, to be witnesses to the end of a life, and seeing with their own eyes something that was once a human being.

The victim's purse was found, and the state trooper found a driver's license in the wallet that he would need for his report, as well as for identification of the victim. Jokes continued sporadically from the tired group of officers gathered around the trooper, but as he flipped through family pictures of the woman and her children, he became very quiet.

The morning light was now growing on the horizon. Slowly, traffic began to flow along once again. EMTs gently placed the victim's body into a waiting ambulance, and a wrecker came to tow away the crashed vehicle. Cars drifted slowly by as drivers craned their necks in an effort to see some piece of the destruction, curious as to what had happened.

The state trooper slowly examined the photographs in his hands. Smiling faces of strangers stared back at him, images of a life taken away, of a family about to be devastated with loss.

"This is so sad," he whispered to himself. Even his dark humor could not protect him, and he turned his face away from the other uniforms.

"I Think He Got Shot"

Sunny Sunday mornings are typically not very busy for police officers. The last of the weekend's festivities have gone away with Saturday night's darkness, and a new day dawns, finding most people heading for church services, relaxing before the coming work week, or sleeping off the over-indulgences from the previous night. Usually, officers can look forward to a fairly calm and uneventful morning.

But not always.

One such sunny Sunday morning, the silence of the radio was broken by dispatchers calling for an officer. A call had come in from a cell phone that a small white car was traveling toward town, weaving erratically; the driver was most definitely drunk. Officers began to move in the direction where the caller was located.

It was, at first, a wild goose chase. The caller on the cell phone would tell the dispatcher where the drunk car was heading, and then the dispatcher would relay the information to the officers. But as the police would turn in that direction, the caller would say that the vehicle he was following had turned a different way. As the officers played their game of zigzag tag, they began to wonder if they would catch the suspect vehicle before the driver either lost them or made it home.

But the cell caller finally told the dispatcher that the car had turned onto a particular road, and one of the officers realized he was right on top of the suspect. Making a turn, he pulled up just behind the small white car, two men inside, as it slowed and stopped in front of a residence.

Walking to the driver's window, the officer immediately noticed that the man in the passenger's seat was acting strange and holding his face in his hands. Leaning down, he was also aware of the smell of alcohol.

"Hello, Sir," he said to the driver, " is everything alright this morning?"

"Well, um, no not really," answered the driver, a dark-haired and bearded man dressed in a T-shirt and jeans. The officer looked more closely at the blond-haired passenger, and saw blood dripping from where his hands covered his face, making an ugly spot on his pants.

"What's wrong with your buddy, there? He looks like he's been injured."

"Oh, yeah, yeah," replied the man nervously. "I think he got shot."

The officer began to be joined by other officers who were arriving on the scene, and all became very concerned at this new revelation. When they examined the passenger, it appeared that a small caliber bullet had indeed passed directly through the bridge of his nose, leaving a painful wound. When the officers asked the injured man how he'd been shot, he kept muttering, "I don't know."

An ambulance was called to the location, and the driver of the white car continued to be questioned. Both men appeared intoxicated, but they were also unusually nervous and vague in their answers as to what had happened. The driver finally told the officers that the two had left a party "somewhere out in the country" and were driving to a friend's house when they "heard a gun shot" and the passenger's side window blew out. But as to exactly where the shooting had occurred, the man could not give a direct answer.

But, some clues were beginning to come to light as the officers took a close look at the men and the car. First of all, they noticed how fearful the passenger seemed of the man who was driving. Second, the passenger's window was indeed blown out, but there was no glass inside the car. If a bullet had been fired through the window from the outside, the interior should have had shards of glass everywhere. Still, when presented with these findings, the men still could not, or would not, say how the shooting had occurred. Officers had their suspicions about the driver, but with no weapon and no statement from the victim, they could only arrest the driver for DUI and charge the passenger with public intoxication.

About a year later, the man who was driving became involved in a fight during a card game, when he was stabbed in the chest and died almost instantly. Afterward, a story began to surface about the Sunday morning shooting.

It seems that the driver was a bit of a "tush hog," who liked to fight, drink, and bully people around. When he and the blond-haired man had gotten into an argument that morning in the car, he pulled out a small handgun and shot his friend through the nose. He threatened the man more, and then threw the gun out the window when he saw he was being followed. The victim was so terrified, he refused to say anything of the incident until after the other man's death.

But, as with many who live their lives to threaten and harm others, the "tush hog" eventually ran into someone who wasn't so terrified.

The Memories Can Weigh Heavily on Emergency Workers

The very nature of the jobs of firemen, EMTs, rescue workers, and police officers demands that they be forced to see and experience things that most people only watch on television. What these people may undergo for hours at a time is condensed for the general public to a four or five second television news video. If you don't like what you see on TV, you can simply turn the channel. Firemen, EMTs, and cops don't have that luxury.

It can be painful, both physically and emotionally, to carry horrible images around in your head for years on end, especially when those experiences can occur so suddenly, with no warning.

A quiet and uneventful shift can quickly turn terrible when a call comes out of a homicide. One minute, you are enjoying a nice midnight lunch with your fellow officers; the next, you are walking through a violent murder scene, placing together the mode and method of a killer and the last seconds of the victim's life. The senselessness and viciousness by which such deeds are often done are incomprehensible, but it is the officer's job to discover the truth in order to prosecute the offender.

Fires can rage unexpectedly. It is difficult to watch a family's home and all their possessions disappear in flames, but even more so when it is confirmed that a victim has perished inside. Someone has to go in and locate the body, and it is almost always the responsibility of a firefighter. Even after risking life and limb in extinguishing the blaze, he was required to walk through a nightmarish scene to come face to face with death.

A good friend of mine, who is a Paramedic, recalls an unsettling experience from a motor vehicle accident where a young man was mortally injured, though conscious. As the medic worked feverishly to save the boy's life, the young man looked into his eyes and said over and over again, "I feel like I'm going to die."

The Medic tried to console and calm the boy as he applied all of his training and tools in an attempt to treat his injuries, but the boy continued to repeat, "I feel like I'm going to die." Even as the Medic worked, the boy became suddenly quiet and died in his hands.

Working a crime such as child abuse is another disparaging situation for police. An officer must examine the child's injuries, question the victim as well as witnesses and suspects, and of course, document all of his findings in a report. While he may work for days to prepare the case for prosecution, the sometimes limited support of human services and the court system may only prolong the innocent child's suffering. It can leave an officer with many angry and sleepless nights, wondering if there was something else he could have done.

But perhaps some of the most haunting memories carried by myself and some other officers and EMTs are those from a certain fatal car accident. It occurred one peaceful, sunny day, when a man driving his sports car too fast on a curvy road lost control and crashed. Since he was wearing no seatbelt, he was ejected from the car as it flipped, and his body landed in a deep culvert along the roadside. As the first ambulances and deputies arrived, bystanders watched as the man breathed his last. The violent crash scene and the sight of the man lying on his back, dead in the bottom of a ditch, was compounded by what we saw written on the man's black biker-style T-shirt. It was an ominous sight that we have never forgotten.

In bold letters, the shirt read, "Hell Bound."

The Words of a Victor, not a Victim

She was tall, with gentle eyes. At the conference, she was introduced as a speaker and as a previous victim of domestic abuse. She stepped up to the podium, already a bit nervous at speaking to the large group. Her hands trembled, but she gripped the sides of the podium tightly to steady herself, and she began.

"Are you a victim of domestic violence?" she asked. "If you are, have you told anyone? How old were you when it started? Were you forty? Were you eighteen? Were you six? Or were you too young to even remember when it began, and to you, it seems like that's the way it's always been."

"I once was a victim. But after years of abuse, I finally got tired of it, and I found help. I took my children, and I left my husband. I blamed myself at having allowed my children to witness it for too long, and finally I had had enough. So I went to court, I got the court orders, the orders of protection, and I got my divorce. I took my kids, and I left him. I was told that if he violated the court order, he would be arrested. It was supposed to be the end of it.

But if you don't already know, the abuse and the victimization never truly end. It will always be there. I found that although I was no longer with my abusive husband, I was still forced to allow my children to visit him. I found out that according to the law, he had rights, too. Even though he was the offender, and he had done all of those terrible things to us, he was able to keep his visitation rights with the kids. And now, if I don't follow the court order, I'm the one who could go to jail. And as much as I would like to have never seen or spoken to him again, I am still forced to stay in contact with him. In some ways, I'm still trapped, and the fear never goes away. He still sees our children, and God only knows what happens when they are with him."

Her eyes had become wet with tears as she continued, "I probably could have kept him away from the children, or at least had his visitation supervised. But I was afraid to tell about some of the things that had happened. I was embarrassed and ashamed. I should have told those things to the attorneys, or the police, or the judge, but I didn't, and I know that now. The laws aren't perfect. He was wrong, and he still has rights. But although I feel like the system has often let us down, I realize my own part in the system's failure. Don't make the same mistake I did. Don't be afraid to tell things.

"Another hardship was the being alone. But I found strength in people who cared about me. I rely on the support of service agencies, my family, and my friends. I met other women who were like me, and I found out that I wasn't alone after all.

"It has been frustrating, and there are still nights that I never stop crying. I will always struggle to live with my past, with the abuse I endured. And I continue to learn to live with my fear of something still happening to my children when they are with him. But I will do it. No matter what it takes, I will make it."

Although she had suffered, it was clear that she had not given up. She had found a certain measure of power, and it was there she had found her strength. She closed with some encouraging words.

"I was once a victim, but I don't consider myself a victim now. I choose to be a survivor. I want to be a victor, and I want to encourage others who are like me to take a stand. I want them to know they can be victors also."

Taking Isaac Away

Following the Children's Services agents through the wet, narrow streets, the police officer gripped the steering wheel tightly and wished that she were anywhere else. She, like the rest of her fellow officers, had no desire to be part of removing a child from an unfit home, but she knew it had to be done. She had read over the court order and was already familiar with the child's mother. The woman was a known crack addict, who routinely abandoned her three year-old son as she satisfied her desire to get high. Their home was little more than a drafty shack with no plumbing or electricity, even though the mother received a sizable monthly relief check.

And so, it was she, the department's only female officer, who was requested by the Children's Services agents to accompany them as they took custody of the boy. She had done a lot of undesirable things as a cop, but things like this were the worst.

The agents pulled up to the dismal shack, and the officer parked her patrol car behind them. The three walked through the trash-filled yard and onto the rickety porch. Dirty diapers were everywhere, along with hundreds of beer cans. One of the agents knocked on the dirty gray door.

The mother answered, dressed in tight jeans and a T-shirt. Her hair was unkempt and wild. With a sour drawl, she said, "What you want now?"

"We need to talk to you," answered the agent. "It's about Isaac."

"What about him?" she answered, looking warily at the other agent and the female officer. A foul odor escaped through the open door, one of filth and unsanitary air. The officer fought the urge to gag as the Children's Services agent explained, as gently as she could, the court order she carried. Immediately, the woman began shaking her head.

"No. No, you ain't takin' my baby away from me. You ain't."

"Please," said the agent, "it's a court order that we must obey.

You have legal rights to challenge it, but now is not the time for this to be difficult."

"No!" yelled the mother as she tried to slam the door. But the officer caught it and held it open, trying to reason with the distraught woman.

"Don't do this," she said sternly. "You are only going to make this worse. You can't have your son back if you are in jail. If you make this difficult, it will only reflect bad on you when you go to court."

The mother's bloodshot eyes were filling with tears. For a second, she held the door, but she saw the futility in resisting and allowed the three other women to come inside. "It just ain't right! This just ain't right...."

The officer was revolted at what she saw. Living conditions so horrid that it was unimaginable a child could possible be allowed to live there. She spied a crack pipe on a table, but chose to ignore it for the moment, for the small and frightened boy came from an adjoining room clutching a dirty stuffed animal.

"What is it, Mama?"

The mother backed away, trembling as she spoke. "Isaac, you got to go with these ladies."

"How come?" The little boy said as he began to cry. "What did I do?"

The officer knelt down and said gently took his hand. "You haven't done anything, sweetie. But these other ladies have to take you someplace else for a while. There will be lots of toys and a warm bed for you there. Your mama will see you in a little while."

The scared little boy looked helplessly at his mother, who turned away mumbling something incoherently. The officer took him up in her arms and handed him to one of the agents. "It'll be all right. I promise."

Crying, he reached his tiny hand out to his mother, but she seemed to ignore him. The agents consoled him as best they could as they walked with him outside to their waiting car, followed by the officer. Glad to be back outside in the fresh air, she prepared to get to her patrol car and leave, when the mother suddenly ran screaming to the agents' car.

"You can't take my baby! You can't take him!" But the officer restrained her as the car drove away with the little boy sobbing tearfully inside.

"You have to let them do this!" yelled the officer. Her anger was rising against the woman for being such a terrible parent, for allowing her child to suffer in such terrible surroundings, and for destroying both her life and the life of her child. But the anger was tempered with pity. No matter how bad a mother she was, she was still the child's mother.

The officer waited until the woman stumbled back into the dirty house before getting into her patrol car. Thoughts of the little boy troubled her. An innocent victim that could not understand what was happening to him. Brushing a tear from her cheek, she quickly drove away.

When Integrity is at Stake

There are very few things that police officers fear. They routinely place themselves in stressful and potentially deadly situations and are called upon to handle dangerous people. Still, most officers consider this simply "part of the job." Complaints and such are accepted and sometimes even expected when an officer is executing his duties.

But one thing that can truly terrify a law enforcement officer is the thought of losing his integrity. A good officer knows that his job is not based upon how fast he can drive, how straight he can shoot, or how good he looks in his uniform. Everything about his success as an officer is based upon the trust and confidence that the public, as well as fellow officers, place in him. Without it, he is reduced to simply an authority figure that wears a gun and a uniform. He is of no value as a protector of society. To an honest cop, this is the worst possible thing that can happen.

Integrity is defined as "uprightness of character; honesty, complete and undivided." These traits, when applied to a public servant, signify a truly upstanding and trustworthy person. Before an officer ever is allowed to wear a badge, he begins his career in law enforcement by taking an oath to be honorable, fair, and truthful. Such virtues are often hard to find in any career, but a dedicated police officer makes the attempt to live them every day. Some officers work for years to be the kind of professional that the public can instill faith in, someone that other people can depend upon and trust. And so it is, when an officer's integrity is taken away, it can destroy him both personally and professionally.

How does it happen? Officers are often subjected to unfounded criticism by those who are unfamiliar with the job of law enforcement, or worse, from those who have no respect for laws and the police to begin with. What becomes dangerous is when good cops have their reputations tarnished by baseless accusations, especially when those accusations come from other people who wear badges. Years of dedication and hard work are suddenly threatened, and the officer's reputation hangs in the balance.

Certainly, all complaints should be looked into, and most officers will agree that the actions of a few "bad cops" tend to tarnish even the good. But when accusations of misconduct are founded upon conjecture, rumors, and innuendo, we should be careful not to condemn a good and honest police officer.

The public expects nothing less than trustworthiness in the officers that protect it. Law enforcement officers, just like ministers, teachers, or other public figures, are held to a higher standard. So long as there is a public demand for good cops, there will always be honest men and women who will be willing to fill those positions.

But, should we cloud the field with mistrust and personal attacks, good officers may become harder and harder to find. The ranks may become quite thin of those with the self-respect and character needed to be a good cop.

It Only Takes One Good Cop

Her body was found dumped in a remote alleyway, some fifty miles from where she'd last been seen alive. Her coworkers had become concerned when she did not show up at her job, and her family could not find her at home. Investigators found that she had been stabbed repeatedly, and had suffered several blows to the head. Her car was found several miles away, abandoned on the roadside.

All the investigators had was a murdered woman from a county fifty miles away. They knew that she had been murdered somewhere else, but there were few fingerprints, little fiber evidence, no weapon, no motive, and no suspect. A motorist driving along the interstate the night she was last seen reported passing a vehicle that matched that of the victim's, stopped on the shoulder. A man and woman appeared to be fighting, and the motorist thought he had seen the man slamming the woman's head into the car door.

A composite sketch was obtained from the witness's brief sighting of the incident. The investigators had little hope to find the murderer. They assumed he was probably a lonely and nameless drifter that no one knew. Two days passed, and no leads developed. It appeared the case had reached a dead end.

But a deputy sheriff returned to work in the county where the woman worked after his two days off. As he prepared for his shift, detectives passed around the sketch of the murder suspect.

The deputy took one look at the drawing and said, "I know this guy."

It seems that the night the woman was last seen, the deputy had been patrolling along the interstate when he came upon a man walking. The man was dressed in an old green army jacket, with scraggly dark hair. It was cold out, and the officer became a little suspicious.

He could have kept driving, not wishing to get out of his warm patrol car to deal with a hitchhiker. He could have just ignored the man or pretend he hadn't seen him. But this deputy was a better officer than that.

He stopped and spoke with the man for a few minutes. The stranger was friendly and claimed he was just passing through, going north. The man did not appear drunk, and the officer found that a warrant check said he was not wanted. The deputy obtained the man's name and date of birth, and just to be safe, he patted him down. Under the jacket, he found something, but since it was not illegal to possess, he allowed the man to keep it before letting him go.

It was a large hunting knife.

Armed with this new information, investigators across the south began a massive effort to find the man the deputy had stopped. In a few days, reports of him began to surface at truck stops in a neighboring state. In less than a week, he had been found and was arrested. When interviewed, the man described in detail how the lady had given him a ride that cold night after he'd talked to the deputy. She began to talk to him about religion, which angered him. He made her stop the car, and when she kept trying to talk to him, he attacked her. After bashing her into the car door and stabbing her, he drove her to the alleyway and dumped her body, then abandoned her car. He later pled guilty to her murder. The stop that the deputy had made that night, simple but thorough, was credited with being the critical factor that broke the case.

Investigators, as well as her friends and family, had feared that they might never find the answers to such a senseless death. They feared a murderer might never be caught and might go unpunished to possibly take another life on another cold and dark night.

Such might have been the case, had it not been for the efforts of one good cop.

A Time to Be Thankful

The deputy's belt seemed overly tight around his waist, even though it had been over an hour since enjoying Thanksgiving dinner with his family. Although he was scheduled to work the holiday, he had found time to take a long lunch at his grandmother's house. Now, he realized he'd eaten way too much and hoped for a calm shift to finish off his day.

But it was not to be.

The call of a traffic accident with injuries came bursting over the radio. The deputy drove toward the scene as more information trickled over the air: two vehicles, someone seriously hurt, needing rescue, possibly a DOA. But the last transmission made him accelerate the patrol car even faster: a child had been thrown from the vehicle.

Several people had already gathered beside the broken car as the deputy pulled to a stop and turned off his siren. Ambulances, rescue, and other officers were only minutes behind him. He walked quickly up to the crash and saw an SUV wrapped around a tree.

"There's a driver in there that's hurt pretty bad," a bystander said, his voice shaking.

"We were told there was a child involved."

The man nodded and pointed. His voice was almost a whisper. "Right there."

The deputy had not noticed the old shower curtain lying beside the SUV, but his spirit sank as he knelt down and lifted up the edge of the makeshift blanket. The still eyes looked upward, lifeless. The deputy lowered the plastic and shook his head. The boy couldn't have been much older that six.

"It's all we could find to cover him with," said the man, his voice still shaking. "We just didn't want..."

"I know, Sir," answered the deputy, "I understand. It's alright, you did the right thing." Noticing movement inside the vehicle, the deputy patted the man on the arm and went to render what aid he could to the injured driver.

Ambulances arrived, and rescue technicians cut the twisted metal from around the driver. A helicopter landed in a field nearby and flew the injured man to a trauma unit in Knoxville. A highway patrolman quietly finished a report and nodded for the EMTs to do the only part of the job they hated. As they placed the boy's body into the back of the ambulance, few words were spoken. The officers, the rescue personnel, and the medics had all either just finished their holiday meal, or had been right in the middle of it when the call had came out. Most had families and children of their own.

The deputy left as the tow truck took away what was left of the SUV. He drove for several minutes, then turned onto a lonely dirt road and stopped along the roadside.

His mind was full of thoughts about the boy's family, who must surely, by now, have been told the worst possible news they could ever imagine. The deputy had seen a lot over the years, but things like this still bothered him. Children weren't supposed to die, especially not on holidays. It just wasn't supposed to happen.

Thoughts drifted to his own family and the meal they had just shared. Had he even noticed his kids above the small talk and the football game on TV? Or had he been too engrossed in the holiday riff raff to do what the day actually called for: *be thankful.* His eyes were full of tears as he dialed his grandmother's number on his cell phone.

"You still there?" he asked his wife when she answered. "I thought I'd come back by for a few minutes."

"You just left a little while ago," she teased. But she sensed something in his voice. "Is everything OK?"

"I'll tell you about it when I get there," he said. Then he added, "Just do me a favor, and tell the kids I love them."

"This Is Where It Gets Bad"

The burglary call sent the officer down a curvy road to a small, unassuming house with a neatly manicured yard. Gravel crunched under the tires as the patrol car stopped in the driveway.

"Control, I'm on the scene," radioed the deputy.

Since it was a burglary and nothing more, the deputy gathered up his clipboard of report forms, a property list, and a camera. Walking to the door, he saw there were no neighbors close by who might be valuable as witnesses. Based on his past experiences, he grimly decided this would probably be another unsolved break-in.

A young man answered the door dressed in jeans, a T-shirt, and a farm tractor hat.

"Good evening, Sir, I'm Officer Croft. Did you report a burglary?"

"Yeah, that's me," answered the young man. "Come on in, and I'll show you what they done."

The deputy followed the homeowner through the house, jotting down notes as the man walked from room to room, pointing to ransacked shelves and drawers. The officer asked a few questions but was intent on recording the man's description of his property. After all, a homeowner knows his home better than anyone else.

After about fifteen or twenty minutes had passed, the man stopped in the kitchen. The deputy continued to scribble his notes, but stopped as the man became oddly quiet. He looked up to see the young man standing in the middle of the room with his hands in his pockets and a rather strange look on his face.

"OK," said the man, "this is where it gets bad."

"What do you mean?" asked the confused officer.

"I shot him."

"You did what?"

"I shot him. They must have been outside when I got home, because when I came inside I saw the house like this. Then I heard someone trying to get in the back door. I grabbed my shotgun and came in here just as they came in. I yelled at them to stop, and it looked like one of them had a gun. So, I shot him."

The deputy walked, wide-eyed, to the back of the room and saw what appeared to be holes where pellets had nicked the trim around the door. He began to get a bad feeling about this simple burglary.

"All right," said the officer with a calm voice, "I don't see a body anywhere. Did they get away?"

"One of them did," answered the man, "but the other one is dead."

"Do you know where he is?" asked the officer. The man nodded.

The deputy followed the young man out into the yard, and as they neared the roadway, the officer began to notice dark spots of crimson on the grass. The man stopped and pointed to a wet area in the middle of the road.

"He fell right there," he said. "That's where I found him lying."

"Where is he now?" questioned the officer incredulously.

"Over there, across the road."

The deputy walked over and looked down a steep embankment. It had begun to grow dark, so he clicked on his flashlight and shined it down the hill. There, at the bottom of the bank, lay a man's body. Making his way down, the deputy saw the man was clearly dead from a wound in his neck.

Climbing back up, he asked the man, "How did he get down there?"

The man shrugged. "I drug him out of the road and rolled him off the side. Then I washed the blood out of the road with a bucket of water."

The officer shook his head in disbelief. "What on earth did you do that for?"

"Because," replied the man, matter-of-factly, "my mother was coming over, and I didn't want her to have to see anything bad."

The officer asked the man to sit in the patrol car. He then took out his radio and called for backup units and a detective.

"I need them out here quick," said the officer over the air. "There's been a shooting, and one victim is deceased."

As he heard other officers rolling toward him, he turned once again to look at the side of the road where the dead thief lay. Just like the thief, the officer's simple burglary had quickly turned from bad to worse.

"Thanks for Ruining My Day, Cop"

The driver of the pickup truck glanced at his speedometer instinctively, a reaction out of habit because on any other day, the patrol cars would be sitting here, near the bridge. The speed limit was 45, and he was doing 60. Normally, he would slow down when he saw the cop car, but today there wasn't one. So he sped onward.

It was a sunny and hot mid-afternoon, like any other summer day. The road was straight and clear, and so it could have happened any number of ways. Perhaps he reached down to push in a CD or glanced down at a magazine in the seat beside him. No one would ever know. Maybe he was simply daydreaming for a few seconds. But a few seconds is all it took. His right front tire left the pavement and rolled into the loose gravel on the shoulder of the road. His first reaction was to jerk the wheel to the left, and he did so with the tires screaming in protest.

Had he been traveling at a rate closer to the speed limit, he might have managed to regain control, but at 60 miles per hour, the truck felt as if it were on ice beneath him. He slid further off of the road, and when the rear tires came back out of the slick grass and on to the pavement, the unthinkable happened. He felt a tremendous jerk as the truck flipped over, and a horrible sound of breaking glass and scraping metal rang in his ears.

He had also neglected to wear a seatbelt, and now his broken body was tossed like a rag doll around inside the cab of the rolling truck. Pain shot through his body and his blood froze as his mind kept screaming, *This isn't happening. This isn't happening.*

Then, he felt himself fly through the air as he was thrown through a broken window, and then the unbearable tearing of flesh against asphalt.

At intervals, blackness passed over him as he lay there. Suddenly, everything was very quiet, only the searing pain reminded him that he was somehow still living. He heard voices and tried to speak. But only a guttural, strangling sound came from his throat. Inside his chest, a warm feeling spread around his lungs, and he found it harder and harder to breathe. His arm was twisted beneath his back, which made his breathing even more difficult. As he faded in and out of consciousness, the faces of his wife and kids appeared in his memory. Scenes of them ran through his mind over and over as his breathing turned to quick gasps. Tears filled his eyes, knowing his wife would be left alone and his kids with no father. In his agony, he felt as if some weight pressed down upon him, and he became enveloped in the darkness that slowly took the pain away. The faces of his family became dim and faded away into nothing. And he was gone.

The blue lights flashing behind him seemed to sting him. Furious, he cursed and swore at the officer who sat behind him, writing on the ticket pad. In his anger at having been stopped for speeding, he had not noticed the officer's attempts to be civil and professional. At the moment, he could only feel humiliated at being stopped like a common criminal. And he hated the cop for it.

Finally, the officer returned with his ticket book.

"I clocked you at 60 miles an hour in a 45 mile an hour zone, Sir," said the officer in an even tone. "I'll have to ask you to sign this citation for both speeding and for failure to wear a seatbelt."

The man jerked the ticket book out of the officer's hands and scrawled his name at the bottom. But his anger only intensified when he saw the cost of the fine.

"Eighty dollars!" swore the man in the pickup. "Are you serious?!"

"That is the fine set by the city, Sir," replied the officer, handing the man his copy of the ticket.

The driver struck the steering wheel with his fists, and swore louder. "I can't believe this! Eighty dollars! I was barely over the speed limit! Don't you have anything better to do? Why don't you go get a real job instead of harassing hard working people like me?! " He considered filing a complaint with the officer's supervisor or maybe calling the newspaper about the injustice of getting the ticket.

The cop stepped back and replaced his pen into his pocket. "Please slow down, Sir. Drive safely."

The man fastened his seatbelt in a flurry of obscene words. Before he drove off, he shook the ticket at the officer's face.

"Thanks a lot! Eighty dollars! I really appreciate this! And my wife and kids will, too!"

The police officer watched in silence as the pickup truck and the furious man sped away into the mid-afternoon sun.

"Maybe they will, Sir," whispered the officer, "maybe they will."

Sometimes, Angels Are in the Right Place at the Right Time

"We've finally got him," grinned the undercover officer. "He's in his apartment right now with a large quantity of narcotics."

The group of police officers sitting around the room listened anxiously. They had been after the drug dealer for some time, and now it seemed they were about to catch him red-handed. Each officer had been called in to take part in the raid, and as the minutes ticked by waiting for the search warrant to be signed, each officer's excitement grew more intense.

"This is a diagram of his apartment," continued the undercover officer, pointing to the drawing on the blackboard in front of them. "We'll go in two groups, one in the front and one in the back. Be sharp. He'll probably try to fight."

"That's OK," called out a muscular detective. "I like to fight, too."

"It's not that simple," said the undercover officer. "We've got information there is a small child at the apartment, also. So use caution, not only for yourselves, but for any innocent kids who can't help where they are."

At that moment, another detective poked his head in the room, waving a piece of paper. "We got the search warrant. Let's go."

Night had just fallen as the two groups of police officers took their positions outside of the apartment complex. For most of them, their excitement had turned to a nervous anticipation. Each officer knew the uncertain events that waited inside the apartment, and each man made his own peace within himself, should things go wrong. The lead officer gave the signal, and the two teams sprinted for their target.

"Police! Search warrant!"

The declaration rang out, followed by the tearing of wood and fabric as the back door disintegrated with the entrance of the team members. As they fanned out inside the apartment, they began to order those inside to get down on the floor. They also saw the drug dealer leap from a chair in the living room and head for the front door.

He never broke his stride as the muscular detective plowed through the front door, leading the other team through. The detective's eyes flashed as he saw the drug dealer heading straight for him. The suspect swung one of his huge fists at the detective's head, but the cop was quicker. The blow struck the dealer in the nose, sending him flying backward, landing on the end of the couch.

The couch, acting much like a seesaw, flipped upward, and something small and pink that had been lying on the other end flew wildly across the room. The officers froze. What had been thrown through the air was a tiny infant wrapped in a pink blanket.

Like time had somehow stopped, the men watched the baby fly higher and higher, almost touching the ceiling. Then it began to drop, falling back toward the hard wooden floor. In the mind of each officer, one cold thought rang out: *I'm too far away to help.*

But behind the muscular detective had been running the undercover officer. He never slowed down as he crossed the floor in front of the other cops, leaping over broken furniture. As the baby fell, the undercover cop stretched out his arms as he slid to a stop in the middle of the living room. The child landed gently into his outstretched arms. It never even woke from its nap.

Betraying his lack of concern for the danger surrounding the baby, the drug dealer continued to fight with the muscular detective. But with the child now safe, the detective turned his full attention to the belligerent criminal in his grasp. Other officers angrily jumped in. It didn't take long to subdue him.

Back at the station, the two teams met for a debriefing session. The operation was evaluated for its good actions, and for those that were not so good. The subject of the infant, not surprisingly, came up. All of the officers agreed they had been lucky and were glad that they had been forewarned of the child being at the apartment. The muscular detective punched the undercover cop in the arm.

"All I know is," he said with amazement, "I've watched football for twenty years. And that was the most beautiful 'fair catch' I've ever seen."

That's What Little Boys Sometimes Do

Traffic had backed up along the two-lane highway, and like everyone else, the deputy drove slowly along in the line of cars. He'd heard no report of an accident, and wondered at what must have been keeping traffic tied up.

As he came closer to where a secondary road intersected with the highway, he saw what was causing the other drivers to stop. Standing on the edge of the highway, just outside of the lanes, was a small boy of about three years old. His round little face peered anxiously at the cars cruising slowly by, and it was clear he was about to cross the roadway.

The patrol car pulled to a stop near the intersection, and the officer approached the little boy.

"Hey, there," said the deputy gently. "What's your name?"

"Scott," said the boy in a quiet but earnest voice. He seemed not at all afraid of either the officer or the traffic driving past them.

"Well, hello, Scott," grinned the deputy, positioning himself in order to grab the child if he dashed out across the pavement. "What are you doing out here by the road?"

The little boy pointed across the highway to a large field, and replied, "That's my dog." Sure enough, the deputy saw a brown collie out in the field, sniffing about, unconcerned for the boy who was following him. But the child's small eyes were fastened on the collie. He looked toward the animal as if it were his best friend.

Little boys intent on following their dogs struck a soft cord inside the deputy. He placed a hand on the boy's shoulder. "It looks like your dog is OK. He's just playing over in the field over there."

The little boy did not appear convinced.

"You know how you don't like to stop playing when you're having fun?" The boy nodded. "Well, he's just having fun right now. He'll come right back to you when he gets tired, right back to your house. Where do you live at?"

The boy pointed a small hand back to a large sloping field behind him, up to a single-wide mobile home. "Up yonder. That's where I live."

"Wow, that's a long way. Did you walk all the way down here by yourself?"

The boy nodded. "Uh-huh. I was followin' my dog."

"You know, I bet your mom might be scared if she doesn't know where you are. Since it's a long way back to your house, would you like to ride in my police car?"

Normally a kid would jump at the chance, but this little boy still stared out across the road at his canine companion. With great hesitance, he finally nodded and walked with the deputy back to the car. The officer was impressed with his devotion to his pet.

They drove down the secondary road and turned up the driveway. Stopping in front of the mobile home, the officer and the boy got out just as the front door sprang open. A portly woman with blonde hair rushed out and ran toward the police car. The deputy noticed the look in her eyes was more of anger than of worry.

"Scott!" she snapped, "what did you do?"

"He was down by the road, Ma'am," said the deputy. The falling tone of his voice was clearly aimed at the inattentive parent. "He was just following his dog, like little boys are sometimes want to do."

The woman glanced at the officer, embarrassed. For a second, the deputy regretted having made the comment, but his regret vanished as she jerked the boy up by the arm and pushed him toward the house. Another young woman and a bearded man were now standing in the doorway watching.

"You get in that house right now! That stupid dog…"

"He ain't stupid," whispered the little boy as he stuffed his hands into his pockets and shuffled toward the trailer.

The deputy came around his car, trying very hard to hide is rage. He said something to the woman, but the words he said were very low, so that only she could hear him. And as he spoke, she drew backward, nodding at what the deputy had spoken of, that if he found out the child were to be harmed in any way, how unfortunate it would be if a report were made to Children's Services, and how many witnesses had seen the child unattended by the highway. He made his point and walked back to his patrol car.

As he drove back out onto the highway, a young man in a pickup truck called out to him as he passed by, "Can you call Animal Control? I almost ran over that stupid dog over there as it was running up to that trailer."

The deputy glared at the pickup and glanced again at the home at the top of the grassy hill. He sighed and whispered three words to himself.

"He ain't stupid."

The Nice Bird Gets the Worm

Tommy was a good ole' boy, a slim, smooth-talking construction worker who drifted from job to job and in and out of trouble with the law. Sometimes a petty thief, he was well known among local police officers.

But one thing about Tommy that most officers agreed on: he was a nice guy. Although his criminal record was as long as a country mile, Tommy never refused to be arrested, never tried to run, and never tried to fight. When he was caught in some sort of criminal activity, he would only try to talk his way out of the mess and go peacefully when his efforts of escape failed.

One officer in particular seemed to be the one who always was working when Tommy got into trouble. It never failed that when Tommy was arrested, it was the same officer that brought him in: a tall deputy who wore glasses and was a generally pleasant personality. He actually liked Tommy and pitied him for the fact that he could have made something of himself if he'd wanted to.

But not every cop liked Tommy. Some were rude to him, considering him to be a low-life. Every now and then, Tommy would be brought in by such an officer who belittled him and gave him every reason to resist arrest. But Tommy never did, choosing simply to bear the insults and go in "the easy way."

One day, Tommy was arrested in another county, and since there were active arrest warrants out for him, Tommy was scheduled to be picked up and returned to his home county. As luck would have it, it was the tall officer in glasses who picked Tommy up for his ride back to the jail. The two talked and joked on the way back.

"So, what did you get picked up for Tommy?'

"Aw, I was drinkin' a little too much. You know how it is."

"Yeah, that's too bad," nodded the deputy. "We've got warrants for you on some theft charges. Two of them."

"I figured as much," answered Tommy from the back seat. "That was some stuff I took from my uncle. Just borrowed it, really. But I forgot to take it back."

"That'll get you every time," laughed the deputy. "You're going to have to try to stay out of trouble."

"Yeah," said Tommy wistfully. He sat silently for a moment. "You know, you've always been pretty good to me."

The deputy glanced in the rear view mirror. "What do you mean?"

"Well, any time you've arrested me, you've always been decent about it. You know, treated me like a person. I can't say that about all the law I've had dealin's with."

The officer shrugged. "It's not my job to mistreat people, Tommy. Besides, you've never given me any trouble, and I appreciate that. You know I'm just doing my job, but you never held it against me. I can't say that about everybody I've arrested."

Tommy nodded, thinking. He looked out the window of the patrol car.

"You see that old barn over there?"

The deputy looked over at the old abandoned barn, surrounded by scrub brush, about 300 feet from the road. "Yeah, I see it. Why do you ask?"

Tommy smiled. "Let's just say you should probably go look in that old barn."

The deputy glanced again in the rear view mirror. "What are you talking about, Tommy?"

"My ex-girlfriend's brother used to own that old barn. Still uses it, if you know what I mean. Me and him never got along. But you've always been a pretty nice person. So just consider this a favor between me and you. When you drop me off, go back and check on that barn."

The deputy nodded. "Alright, Tommy. I'll do that."

After leaving Tommy at the jail, the deputy drove back to the old barn off the highway. It took several minutes to negotiate a path through the overgrown weeds and brush around the barn, but he was finally able to get to the barn door. With a push, it swung open.

"Well, well."

Inside, buckets of full-grown marijuana plants lined the walls and filled the old stables. Under an old piece of canvas, several home electronic items were found, which he guessed were probably stolen. As he pulled out his radio to call for some assistance to help him with his discovery, he remembered the compliments Tommy had paid him, and he remembered that nice guys don't always finish last.

Two Graves in Greenhill

Part 1

In Greenhill Cemetery just south of Etowah, Tennessee, there are two graves among the rows of granite headstones that might not draw much attention from the casual passerby. They are the final earthly resting places of two men, well known in Etowah, and although their graves are separated by some 200 feet, their lives, and their deaths, are connected.

It was an early spring day in April 1947, when Charles Dunn rode into Etowah on his motorcycle. The big black bike was loud enough to attract the attention of young women who were shopping and walking the sidewalks of Tennessee Avenue. Charles was easily recognized, a local young man who liked to be seen. He made a few stops, and wound up in the "Hole-in-the-Wall Bar." The Hole-in-the-Wall was one of many "beer joints" that graced Etowah's Main Street and consisted of a narrow hallway with a bar on one side and just enough room for a row of barstools on the other. The place was full of men, some having a few drinks with friends, others discussing the current political problems in McMinn County, others simply getting drunk. Charles walked in, smiling, glad to be among the rough crowd he enjoyed being part of. He sat at the bar and ordered a drink.

A few seats away, a slim, older man with dark eyes sat talking with a short, gravel-voiced railroader. As soon as Charles Dunn entered the bar, the older man had taken note of him, his dark eyes darting around the room, always aware of who was around and what they were doing. It was a trait that had served him well some twenty years earlier as Sheriff of McMinn County, and as a U.S. Marshall. His name was T.B. "Burkett" Ivins.

Ivins didn't care much for Dunn. It wasn't uncommon for Ivins to feel as such, for the number of people he trusted was small. Ivins was his own man, had always been. Whether it was as a lawman or running moonshine off the top of nearby Starr Mountain during prohibition, Burkett Ivins lived his own life as he wanted, looking to no other man to justify his actions. He'd shot men before, killed at least one, and had the reputation of a man not to be trifled with. He was now in his sixties, but most people still feared him, except a young, reckless man like Charles Dunn. To Dunn, Ivins was just an old man who people seemed to tiptoe around for no reason. Maybe that was what bothered Burkett Ivins the most.

In the Hole-in-the-Wall that spring day, Dunn was loud and boisterous. Ivins, a man of few words, let it be known that he didn't care much for Dunn, and on that point, he was very specific. Dunn, younger and refusing to back down, made statements to Ivins that might be considered threatening. The railroad man and a few other patrons stepped between the two, trying to calm the situation down. Most of the older men were familiar with Ivins's reputation. For a few minutes, everything seemed to be all right. Then, Dunn made one last belligerent remark toward Ivins and got up to leave.

Ivins quietly finished his drink, paid his tab, and walked out of the bar. His long legs carried him off the sidewalk and onto the edge of Tennessee Avenue where he stood face to face with Charles Dunn.

Some say that in the bar, Charles had threatened Ivins's life. Others say it was a threat toward his family, and still others say that Dunn was armed. In court testimony later, Ivins would swear that Dunn had picked up a brick and was coming at him. But one thing was for sure: Burkett Ivins was always armed. And that spring day, he drew his pistol and shot Charles Dunn dead on Tennessee Avenue in Etowah. A small boy witnessing the killing ran to his father's lumber company a few blocks away.

"Daddy," he said, out of breath and with wild eyes, "Burkett Ivins just shot a man. I saw him do it." His father took him roughly by the arm and said, "You don't say a word about this. You didn't see a thing, you hear? This is something a boy don't need to get involved in."

Moments later, the boy watched as Burkett Ivins sped around the corner of the block, heading toward his home on 7th Street. He could hear the crowd on Tennessee Avenue, someone calling for a deputy.

The little boy, remembering his father's admonition, wondered at what a terrible thing he had seen and what terrible things might still follow because of it.

Two Graves in Greenhill

Part 2

Several months went by in the violent summer of 1947, with the citizens of Etowah and East Tennessee shocked by the shooting of Charles Dunn by T.B. "Burkett" Ivins. Dunn's family called for justice, but for them, the process was painfully slow. Too slow, perhaps.

To people who were familiar with Burkett Ivins, the shooting had come as no surprise. Ivins had been at odds with the Dunns for some time, especially Charles, who Ivins had a particular dislike for. Some even said it was a dislike motivated by politics, some said it was motivated simply by fear. For although many people feared the ex-law man and moonshiner, Burkett Ivins, he had his own ghosts as well. He'd made many enemies during his lifetime, and he knew that there were some people who would just as soon see him dead. Ivins was a man who constantly looked over his shoulder, always cautious of anyone around him.

His caution was a well-known characteristic. On any given day, Ivins would drive to downtown Etowah, get out of his car, step up to the alley way beside Cantrell Bank, and stand with his back to the wall, watching people pass by, and speak to those he knew. Ivins never allowed people to gather behind him.

A trial was held in the county seat of Athens with Ivins accused of murdering Dunn. After a long deliberation, the trial ended with a hung jury. Friends and family of Ivins were happy at the trial's conclusion, insisting that he'd fired in self-defense. Acquaintances of the Dunn family were less than pleased he'd not been convicted and whispered that things were not finished.

Summer passed, and as the autumn leaves began to turn, much of the discussion around Etowah's diners and beer joints centered on the Dunn shooting. Many people waited and wondered about the crime, curious as to how the situation would "play out" with Burkett Ivins. For Ivins, himself, life went on as usual. He left his house every morning to drive downtown, often accompanied by his five-year-old grandson, Danny.

One October day as the little boy walked across his grandfather's yard, Danny was startled by Burkett's guard dogs barking at him from near the garage. Intending more for the boy not to be frightened rather that his home be guarded, Ivins took the dogs away from the house that evening, out to his property in the country.

The next morning, Ivins led the small boy out of the big house on 7th Street, out to the garage, and placed him in the big Ford Coupe. Danny climbed into the seat where he liked to stand at his grandfather's shoulder. Ivins closed the car door and pressed the starter button.

The inside of the car turned into a fireball as a bomb placed on top of the engine exploded, tearing through the dashboard and into Burkett and the small boy. Danny, perhaps shielded by his grandfather's body from most of the blast and shrapnel, was knocked almost unconscious as the car was ripped apart around him. Stunned, injured, and in shock, he slumped over onto his grandfather's body. Still living, but knowing his injuries were mortal, Ivins reached out with a trembling and bloody hand and pushed open the passenger door that was already hanging at an odd angle from its top hinge.

"Get out, Danny," he said quickly, barely able to breathe. "Get out." The boy, his small hand mangled, his body still in shock, barely moved.

"Danny!" barked Ivins, his voice loud but weak, "Danny, get out." He reached over and helped the boy across the tattered and smoking seat, through the open door and onto the ground.

The explosion was heard all over town, and neighbors rushed to the scene. Police and an ambulance arrived that took the boy to a nearby Doctor's office. As the doctor tended to the boy's hand, his grandfather was rushed to Athens in a vain attempt to save him. Knowing the end was near, Ivins told the doctor tending him, "Just give me something, and let's get this over with." The figure of a man larger than life, a man that so many people either feared or respected, loved or hated, died minutes later. The incident caught the attention of regional papers, and people all across East Tennessee gathered, in earnest, to pray in concern over the severely injured boy. When it was learned that Danny would survive, a Knoxville paper fifty miles away printed the headline: *Danny Lives!*

As there was no trial for the death of Charles Dunn, there would also not be one for the death of Burkett Ivins. An investigation into the car bombing of one of the town's most well known citizens resulted in only suspects, but no convictions.

And so the two men have rested in the Greenhill Cemetery for over fifty years, and the mystery of their story remains. Their headstones and the story behind their deaths are a sad reminder of the "dangerous times" of the '30s and '40s, as so many aged people refer to the period. And only an occasional whisper is made of the two men whose graves both lie in the same section of Etowah's Greenhill Cemetery, and whose lives came to violent ends in the spring and fall of 1947.

Part Three

It's easy to make assumptions about a person or a group of people until you've walked in their shoes. This section is about people, and their reactions to what happens to them. Sometimes strange things happen, and sometimes ordinary people rise to the occasion and become heroes.

Think Before You Complain About the Police

Police officers are public servants, but the duties performed by law enforcement officers are often at odds with the expectations of the public they serve. What seems right or acceptable to an officer in a certain situation can sometimes seem wrong in the view of the public. Even though officers are trained a certain way, citizens can and do take offense at the methods officers use to do their jobs, even when the officer is simply using his training to ensure his own safety.

Communities want to live in peace, without fear of danger or trouble from lawbreakers. With those desires in mind, we want our police officers to be constantly alert for criminal activity, and we want them to investigate suspicious activity and to do whatever is necessary to catch the offender. We expect officers to protect us from the criminal element, even if we really don't know who the bad guy is. Toward criminals, we expect officers to be stern and diligent, taking a tough stand against the evil people of society.

But when we, who consider ourselves good citizens, suddenly find ourselves in situations where an officer is questioning our conduct, our opinions change. People sometimes complain that an officer was "cold" or "rude," or that they were made to feel like they had "done something wrong." Whether it is a traffic stop, an encounter with an officer on the street, or sometimes simply an officer's presence, we seem to be easily offended by what the officer says or does. Often, we become uncomfortable. Our anger flares, and sometimes we are rude to the officer, or worse yet, we file a complaint with the police department that expresses our dismay at being treated "like a criminal."

One of the more common responses from people after receiving a traffic ticket is: "Why don't you leave good citizens alone and go catch some real criminals?" But if we see a car driving the least bit fast on our roadways, one of the first things we do is to look around and see if the police are near so they can stop the car and give them a ticket! We expect the police to enforce all laws equally against every person, unless that person is us.

Any other group of people can gather together to have a relaxing lunch, but let several patrol cars be seen at a restaurant and the opinion is that they are "loafing." They are constantly observed driving too fast on the highway, but are berated for being too slow to arrive when we call them. It can be frustrating to officers to have so many conflicting demands from the public. Especially when joe citizen sees something he doesn't understand and assumes the worst of an officer.

A case in point is a situation that occurred not long ago. Two officers received a call to respond to a fight at a well known residence. It was departmental policy to respond quickly to such a call, since the likelihood of violent injury or death is increased in a domestic situation. The two patrol cars went racing to the scene with blue lights flashing, passing several cars along the way. But about halfway to the residence, dispatchers radioed the officers to disregard the call. The complainant had just reported the offenders involved in the fight had left the scene. The two officers slowed down, turned off their blue lights, and pulled their patrol cars into a convenience store to buy a Coke.

But one of the cars they had passed was driven by a prominent local citizen. He had seen the two police cars zoom by and had seen the blue lights. But as he passed the convenience store, he saw the officers casually entering the establishment as if nothing was wrong. He drew a hasty conclusion, based on his limited information, and he became angry at what he thought he was seeing. That afternoon, he called the department and filed a formal complaint, saying he had seen the two officers driving like maniacs with their blue lights on simply to get to a convenience store "so they could socialize." He said that, as a citizen, he was offended at the officers' behavior and expected something to be done about it. Needless to say, the two officers were completely oblivious as to why they were accused of such behavior, and quickly explained to their supervisors what had happened. No action was taken against the officers.

But there might have been, if the supervisor, chief, or sheriff had second-guessed the officers' actions. Even though they were operating completely within all laws and regulations, that simple and misinformed complaint could have damaged the records of two good men.

While police officers should certainly be responsible for any and all duties they perform, citizens are also responsible. After all, if citizens trust officers enough to expect nothing but professionalism when dealing with crime, we should trust that officers are dealing with us professionally as well. Before complaining or accusing, it often helps to become familiar with an officer's job. And simply giving public servants the "benefit of the doubt" can go along way.

"With Sorrow and Few Regrets"

Shady Grove Baptist Church sits under the shadow of Starr Mountain, just inside Monroe County, Tennessee. It is not difficult to see the American flag flying over the Church Cemetery on the nearby hill as one passes by on Highway 39 East. But on closer inspection, a large tombstone can be found standing beneath the flag snapping in the stiff breeze. The stone is six feet high and four feet wide, and on it are inscribed the last words of an American hero.

With our country presently engaged in a war, and many of our service men and women thousands of miles from home during the holidays, we should continue to be conscious of their sacrifices. Fighting a war like no other, against an enemy like we have never faced before, our troops must understandably be under stress from both the dangers they face as well as from the separation from family, friends, and home. For the soldier, a terrible part of war is not knowing if you will ever make it home alive again. Some of our servicemen have already made that supreme sacrifice. There may be more before this conflict is finished.

Danny Roberts made that sacrifice some thirty-two years ago in Vietnam, on February 4, 1970. A young, good-looking country boy from McMinn County, only recently graduated from Central High School, was drafted during the Vietnam War. Eleven months later, Danny was killed while on patrol. Like so many other young soldiers, he gave his life in the service of his country. His ties to his family and home were very tight, even though he was half a world away. Knowing the possibility of losing his life, Danny gave a letter to his best friend, which was not to be opened except in the event of his death. When his parents received the saddening news that Danny had been killed, the family gathered together and read Danny's letter. In it were these words, which today can be found inscribed in stone at Danny's grave:

I want this put on a large tombstone at the head of my grave:

To whom it may concern,

I lived in this here climate for 20 years, the first 19 were full of excitement and pleasure, then it happened, I got drafted and sent to fight a useless war. With God's help I'll make it to heaven, I've spent my time in hell. Take heed dear friends, I died needlessly, along with a lot of my comrades, but I did my best. This is a cruel world that we live in. Even though, I consider myself the luckiest guy in the world because of you my many dear friends and relatives and because I had the greatest mom and dad in the world. Goodbye for now. We'll meet again on that great judgment morning. May God bless and keep all of us and bring everlasting peace.

Danny R. Roberts

My last wish let it be done. Goodbye mom and dad. Goodbye my dear friends, I loved you all so much.

This ain't the end, it's only the beginning. I leave you with sorrow and few regrets. See you all again with God's help.

After thirty years, it seems our world is still as cruel. Young people still are called to fight, and sometimes to die, for their country. Just like Danny Roberts, who grew up in the same hills that I did, and who played football on the same high school field where my friends and I did, and who walked in line behind my mother at their high school graduation. Young heroes like Danny, who in only eleven months, was promoted several times, earned three purple hearts, and received a bronze star. Young people with the same fears, the same love for family and friends, the same loneliness in being so far away from home. But the men and women in our armed forces now engaged in Afghanistan do so because they know it is their duty. That is the mark of heroes. Heroes like Danny Roberts.

It is a duty they do "with sorrow and few regrets."

To Simply Write is Not Enough

I had been a writer for only a few years when I realized writing wasn't everything.

It had been a good year for me, the best so far. I had managed to add my syndicated weekly column to another newspaper, had published two articles nationally, and had published two books. I was beginning to see the possibility of becoming a full-time writer, a dream that few ever attain.

While searching for a subject for a new column, a search that haunted me each and every week, I came across a human interest story about a soldier killed in Vietnam who had written a letter to his parents outlining his funeral arrangements and recording his last words. The act had become somewhat of a local legend, due to the fact that his family had the entire letter inscribed on a six by four foot headstone. With the many of our soldiers being sent to Afghanistan, engaged in the war against terrorism, I thought the subject appropriate.

I was familiar enough with the story to write the article, but I felt the need to speak with his family before I published it. I wasn't even sure if his parents were still living, but after a few phone calls, I located them and arranged a visit. I was surprised to find that the now elderly couple lived only a few blocks from my home.

When the day arrived, I printed off a copy of the article and went to the home of the soldier's parents. They welcomed me in, we made small talk, and I presented them with the column.

It had been almost thirty-two years since the day their world came apart. The memories of their lives before that day were contained in black and white photographs, letters, and newspaper clippings. It surprised me that they could speak of those painful days as easily as they did. Only a few times did I see his mother's eyes become dim with tears, but she would quickly wipe them away and continue with our talk.

"I don't know how he did it," said his mother, referring to the letter her son had written. "I didn't think he could ever do anything like that. We had no idea he had written all of it until after he'd died. He gave it to his best friend who brought it to us. The whole family gathered together when we read it."

His father shared more with me when I asked about Danny as a young man.

"He never liked black people, you see," said his father. "We had lived in several different places before segregation, and Danny had never known any blacks. When he was in high school, he just avoided them, kept away."

"Even in the service, he did," his mother continued. "The black boys who were with him told us that when we saw them at the reunions. Said they knew Danny didn't like them when he first went over there. But then one of them told us how one day they were being shot at, and it so happened that he and Danny dove into the same foxhole. Danny said, 'They're trying to kill us!' And the other boy said, 'Tell me about it.' From then on, they were real good friends. It didn't matter what color a person was over there."

"Another black feller, he was sort of small-built, he talked about Danny, too," added the father.

"Oh, yes," continued his mother, "he said that when they would march up those mountains, Danny would take his pack and carry it for that boy. Danny would write us about his 'soul brothers.' Those boys got close over there." I could see from everything they said that Danny had been a leader. The testimony of his comrades proved it.

They told me more about their son's fellow soldiers. The man who was walking behind him that day on patrol when Danny was killed had sent them a Christmas card every year since that day. Others wrote or visited each year, even though they lived throughout the country. It was clear how much those other men meant to the parents of the dead soldier: the only link to what was, and what might have been.

I asked about a frame full of medals that hung on the wall.

"Oh, yes, those are all Danny's," answered his father. I looked closer and saw not one but three purple hearts, a Bronze Star, and others. "He was wounded two other times and never even told us. He was only in the Army for eleven months, but was about to be promoted for the third time when he got killed. He was shot right through the forehead."

The conversation moved back and forth, from their son, to people in the community we all knew, to my family and myself. I mentioned my three small sons, not thinking much of the statement at the time. We looked at more pictures, and both of them seemed genuinely appreciative of my article. I thanked them, embarrassed that I had initially considered the subject only something to write about, something to keep the editors off my back until the next week. But I had found that simply writing the words was nothing. The creating of this article, this story, had more meaning than I had imagined. It was clear when his mother said to me, "When someone does something like you've done, it's almost as if Danny is still alive. Almost as if he's still having an effect on people. People will still know him and remember him."

I finished with my notes and was preparing to leave, when his father presented me with a copy of the original letter their son had written. I had copied the letter from the tombstone a few days earlier, but this gift, written in the young man's own hand, is still priceless to me. Holding it, I felt connected to him like never before. I saw in myself the same fears and concerns he must have experienced as he wrote those words. Then his mother told me this: "You take good care of those boys of yours." Her eyes never left mine as she spoke, a tiny tremor in her voice. "You just don't know. You never know."

And there it was. Her pain, her loss, all combined into only a few words. Words of admonition for me, a warning, and advice. Motherly advice. I could almost hear my own mother and father saying those same words to a writer who came to their house to talk about the son they had lost, or could have lost, if fate had been different. But fate had been kind to my family. And simply writing about this family's loss had not been enough. It was the look in their eyes when they spoke of him. The sound in their voices as they called his name as if he were still there.

And in a story that was published a few days later, he was. In the hearts and minds of every reader in every corner of the world the story was sent, Danny lived on, a hero again. Writing wasn't everything. Meaning and knowing what I had written was a treasure I would never forget.

Times When Even the Good Guys Want to Lie

It is difficult to describe the emotions that civil servants feel when they are called upon to do things and see things that most other people only hear about. Whether it is a Fire Fighter, Paramedic, Emergency Medical Technician, Rescue technician, Police Officer, or Deputy Sheriff, some on-the–job experiences are difficult, if not impossible, to deal with. Civil servants do jobs that are highly stressful, often dangerous, and have very little pay or benefits. Add all that to the emotional baggage of feeling underappreciated by the people they serve, and it can be a lonely and difficult career for those who manage to last.

I receive a lot of compliments about the things I do, mostly because I am increasingly in the public eye from my writing. I really appreciate those comments, and there have been times when that person who said something positive to me about my job did more for me than they could ever know. There are many more civil servants out there, most who are much better at what they do than I am. The following is a version of a very moving poem, written anonymously, that I received a few weeks ago. It relays the feelings civil servants experience when they want to shield victims and offenders from the truth but know they cannot. This holiday season, don't forget those men and women who keep the roads safe, protect your lives, and save you and your property when it is endangered. A few kind words can go a long way.

"I Want to Tell You Lies"

I want to tell this little boy his mom will be just fine
I want to tell that dad we got his daughter out in time
I want to tell that wife her husband will be home tonight
I don't want to tell it like it is, I want to tell them lies.

You didn't put their seatbelt on,
You think you killed your kids
I want to say you didn't,
But in a way you did
You pound your fists into my chest,
You're bursting so inside
I want to say you'll be OK,
I want to tell you lies.

I see you crying as your life goes up in smoke
If you'd maintained that smoke alarm,
You're children may have woke
Don't grab my arm and ask me if
your family is alive,
Don't make me say those words I must,
I'd rather tell you lies.

I want to say that she's OK, you didn't take her life.
I hear you say you love her and you'd never hurt your wife.
You thought you didn't drink too much,
You thought that you could drive.
I don't want to tell the truth this time,
I want to tell you lies.

But I have to tell it like it is, until my shift is through.
And then the real lies will begin, when I come home to you.
You ask me how the day was, I say it was just fine.
I hope you understand, sometimes,
I have to tell you lies.

This One's for You, Chief

Eleven years ago, Hershel Jack trusted me enough to give me a badge, a uniform, and a gun. It was the beginning of my career in law enforcement and public service, and had he not given me that opportunity so many years ago, I daresay my life would have been very different.

He was the Chief of Police in Englewood, Tennessee, my hometown. He knew who I was and knew some of my family, but he must have taken a lot of confidence in me and the other young officers back then. In fact, almost all of those offices are still working in law enforcement, and those who are not, still work in some field of public service. I wonder what our county would be like now if Hershel Jack had never given those men the chance to be police officers.

Besides being my boss at both the Englewood Police Department and the Sheriff's Department, Hershel was my friend. Sometimes he was difficult to deal with, and I had my share of long talks with him over some action he thought I should or should not have taken as a deputy. Hershel had it in his mind the way he wanted things to be, and woe to the officer that did not live up to his expectations.

But complaints are often filed against officers, some valid and some trumped up. Should such a concern reach Hershel, he was fond of inviting the person who filed the complaint in to meet with him and the officer in an effort to resolve the conflict. It has been my experience that not every supervisor will support his officers, but that was far from the case with Hershel Jack. So long as he believed you were in the right, he trusted you. He had faith in your integrity. In all my dealings with false accusations made against the department, I never saw Hershel turn against an officer's word. Never, not once, did I see him fail to support his men when they were right. Even so, he always treated people as people, and it was rare that a citizen (or an officer) left his office feeling they had been treated unfairly.

He was a cop for a long time and was full of stories about things he had seen and experienced. He could tell a story, and most people know he liked to tell them. I have several in my memories that will likely appear in these columns someday.

When Hershel Jack passed away, suddenly, in May of 2000, our community lost a fine man. Even in retirement, he was active in civic activities as well as in the Republican Party. Not that party lines meant much to Hershel when he chose his friends. Once, he told me that a "big Republican" had expressed displeasure at seeing Hershel display a picture of Tennessee Bureau of Investigations Director Larry Wallace, a long-time Democrat, on his office wall. Hershel pointed proudly to the picture and said, "You know, things like that don't matter to me. The man in that picture is my friend, a good friend, and that's all that's important."

I will always remember him like that: dedicated to the people around him. He was forever dedicated to and concerned for his community, and no matter what social standing, race, religion, political party, or creed, Hershel gave you every ounce of fairness that he could. When something was important to him, he did not hesitate to speak up and take a stand, even when that stand was unpopular or misunderstood.

To use one of his own phrases, "I said that to say this: that man was always good to me."

This one's for you, Chief.

It's Wise to Be Wary of "Unloaded" Fireams

Gun control is and has been a topic of hot debate over the past several years. I have my own opinions on gun control, but I personally believe that gun safety is a much more important subject. After all, guns are a part of our lives here in the South no matter what our opinion of them may be. Everyone needs to be aware of and practice good firearm safety, especially gun owners.

Many people, fearful of crime and bodily injury, go out and purchase a firearm without ever learning how it works or what it could do. A certain lady I am familiar with found herself the owner of a shotgun, but was so intimidated by it that she never took it out of its box. That is, until she heard a noise in her home one night. In a panic, she took out the shotgun and roamed through her home, Rambo-like, to investigate the cause of the strange noises. She found nothing, of course, although she must have been a menacing sight carrying around that unloaded shotgun with the manufacturer's paper tags still hanging off of it.

As a young boy, my father always taught me to be respectful of the rifles and shotguns we hunted with.

"Unloaded guns kill more people than guns that are loaded," he has always said, "because people think a gun is unloaded when it's not." The many hours of firearms training I received as a police officer compounded on this attitude toward safety. But unfortunately, many other people have never been educated in these matters.

Take, for example, a call that another officer and I responded to several years ago. A man had taken his dog outside early one morning, and had slipped a small caliber handgun into his pants pocket in case he "came up on any wild animal or something." While he stood watching his dog, he held the gun in his pocket with a finger on the trigger. When a cat ran across his yard and startled him, he involuntarily jerked his finger and sent a bullet into the inside of his groin.

Extremely lucky that he was not more seriously injured, he was a little embarrassed at the whole incident. This was apparent by the fact that when we arrived he had taken the time to shower and shave and was reclining peacefully on his bed under the stern and watchful eye of his wife.

Alcohol consumption tends to dramatically reduce a person's concern for gun safety. Many times, I, and other officers, have responded to accidental shootings that stemmed from a drunk being in possession of a gun.

For example, a man had partied all night with his wife and some friends. As the dawn began to appear, the guests had evidently worn out their welcome. The intoxicated man picked up a shotgun and threatened, not only his guests, but his wife as well. He stumbled outside, waving the gun around while everyone warned him that he was going to get hurt. Then he started to laugh.

"Oh, I was just tryin' to scare you," he said, "This thing ain't even loaded."

It was about that time that the gun went off.

We arrived to find the man being treated by EMTs in his living room. He was delirious from the alcohol and the pain, and he kept crying that he couldn't find his toes.

We found them outside, in the other half of his shoe.

It is a sobering fact that officers have gone to many other scenes where someone was, in fact, seriously injured or had lost their life because of a disregard for firearm safety. Gun ownership places a great deal of responsibility on a person. Without gaining the proper knowledge of how a firearm works and how to use it safely, it might be easy to wind up in one of the same situations as above.

Don't be a joke, a statistic, or an invalid. Handle firearms safely or don't handle them at all.

Our Sense of Place

There has been much written about the "sense of place" that we feel here in the South. It is a preoccupation with home-places and areas that define us and help us know who we are. More than sentimentality, it is a deeper attachment to family and heritage, even history. It is a part of the rugged individuality that still exists, a hold over from our Appalachian Mountain roots. Some say that the idea of "sense of place" has been overanalyzed, that too much has been written about it. Some would go so far to say that it might never have existed at all.

But a sense of place does exist, even now, here in the beginning of the twenty-first century. Even as our culture becomes more and more blended and similar due to the influences of TV and the Internet, some evidences of our Southern cultural past are still present, although we sometimes don't realize it.

Take traffic fatalities, for example. When a fatal crash occurs on our local streets or highways, it is a public spectacle. Whether we like to admit it or not, most people will slow down and peer at the carnage, somehow entranced by the scene of death. What often happens, days or weeks later, is a cross will appear along the roadside at the sight of the accident, usually placed by family or friends of the deceased. The crosses are often adorned with flowers, cards, and even the name of the victim. One such memorial, recently seen in McMinn County, is quite moving. It marks the location where a young boy was killed a few years ago, and it is topped with a high school graduation cap. We somehow feel we must mark these places, that curve in the road, or that stretch of highway, where someone close to us was taken away. I am told that this phenomenon occurs to such a large extent only in the South.

Our sense of place evolves from a sense of bonding that was once very strong among Southern Appalachian people. Before TV and telephones, we were relatively isolated in our mountains and foothills, and we tended to depend more upon our neighbors than we do now. Our increasingly fast-paced lifestyles have taken away time spent in casual interaction with our neighbors, and sometimes even our families. Still, certain things still show our attachment to our communities and our respect for people.

Funeral escorts have generated a lot of heated debate recently, which brought up the subject of stopping along the roadside when a funeral procession passes. Many people have thought it was "the law" that directed us to stop, and they were surprised to learn that no such law exists in Tennessee. It is simply a tradition to show respect for the deceased and the bereaved family. Again, it is a phenomenon that only appears in the South, mostly in rural areas.

When I would come home from college, I remember noticing how the closer I got to the hills of East Tennessee, the more people would wave at me from their cars as I passed them on the highway. People who didn't even know me would throw up a friendly hand, and I returned the gesture. The late Herschel Jack told me that I should always wave to citizens I passed when driving a patrol car. He was a firm believer that such a minute act kept people feeling close and friendly, especially near an election year.

Even as the habit seems to be fading from our roads and highways, I'm convinced he was right. That stranger waves because it is polite, and to let you know that you are in a good place. You are home.

The Unspoken Understanding

A few weeks ago I attended my friend's funeral. There were many people there, as I knew there would be. He knew a lot of people, and he was one of those unique men who leave an impression on you that you won't soon forget.

My friend's name was Gary Smith. He was a cop.

I have probably written over fifty thousand words this year in stories and articles. I pride myself on crafting the right words to bring my readers into my world, to introduce them to things they might not otherwise see. But finding the words to describe Gary is a bit of a challenge.

He was a textbook cop, like the kind you often see on TV. He smoked like a tar kettle. As long as I knew him, he was physically overweight, had numerous health problems, rarely exercised, and lived on a diet of soft drinks and cheeseburgers while he rode around in patrol cars, chasing bad guys. Some people found him crude. He was disciplined more than once over bad decisions. But he was a cop, and a good cop, at that.

As a police officer, I often found myself in bad situations that were more than a little frightening. But then Gary would get there, and I knew without a doubt I had a good man behind me. If you had to fight the very Devil, Gary was the kind of guy who would be right there with you, holding onto his horns. Not once did I ever second-guess his determination to go into the worst scene imaginable with me. The madder he got, the wider his eyes would get. A few times he would delve into a tirade of swearing that would embarrass a sailor. Well, maybe more than a few times. But as a young officer, I always felt safe with Gary, even when he sometimes was very blunt about a mistake I had made.

"If you ever do that again," he'd say between puffs of cigarette smoke, "I'll shoot you, myself." Then he'd smile, like he was kidding. Sometimes, I'm not sure if he was kidding or not.

But, one thing about Gary that made him a truly good cop was his ability to talk to anybody. He never seemed to consider anyone a stranger. Nobody was too good for him to strike up a conversation with, and certainly no one was beneath him. He pretty much treated everybody he met the same.

At his funeral, the building was crowded with badges and uniforms from a wide range of agencies. There were local and state police, human services, lawyers, district attorneys, parole officers, government officials, business owners, fire departments, and even a preacher or two. The crowd milled about, visiting among each other in that most uncomfortable of situations. They passed through the chapel, offering kind words to Gary's family. As the night progressed, the uniforms tended to gather together in one corner of the building. I've seen it happen at the funerals of other cops.

They talked in muffled tones to each other, their uniforms stiff and crisp. Over their hearts, each man and woman wore their badge. Over their badge was worn a black piece of material. It signified their loss of a coworker, a brother, a father, and a friend. Sometimes, only cops understand other cops. To them, a man's worth is judged by his dependability, by his courage, and by his willingness to stand beside you.

So, in their own way, they stood for Sergeant Gary Smith. They stood along the walls, lined the hallways, and nodded to each other with the unspoken understanding that a good man was gone.

Looking for Answers at an Accident Scene

A report of a motor vehicle accident had been logged in for over an hour before the deputy was finally able to arrive at the scene. It had been one of those nights when everything seemed to be happening at once: bar fights, suspicious persons, burglaries, and any number of reported crimes had been dispatched. Officers had been two and three calls behind all evening. Now, just after midnight, a patrol car pulled up to the hour-old accident scene.

Actually, he was not the first officer there. A patrolman from a nearby town had arrived first, but since the wreck had occurred outside of his jurisdiction, he had simply directed traffic while awaiting the deputy's arrival.

"Glad you finally made it," he told the deputy. "This one's a little strange, since we can't seem to find the driver."

The deputy looked over the scene and saw a badly damaged sport utility vehicle sitting in the middle of the roadway. The evidence seemed clear enough: skid marks told how the vehicle had come around a curve, slid off the road up a small embankment, and flipped over several times before coming to rest. He looked inside the truck and saw that although part of the top was crushed in, the area of the driver's seat had little damage. A pair of men's glasses and a cell phone lay in the rear floorboard. He surmised that if the driver was wearing a seatbelt, he probably survived with little injury. Still, all of the rear windows were broken out. The deputy motioned to some rescue squad personnel who stood nearby.

"Let's do a search of the area, just in case we've had an ejection."

People fanned out over the field on the north side of the road while others climbed the steep embankment on the other side. It was a good rule of thumb to search a 100-foot circle around a wreck scene, and if there were any victims ejected, then articles of clothing would likely be found in that area, which would lead to the victim's body. The officer and the rescue technicians shined their flashlights even farther out, but to no avail. They saw nothing.

"Probably a drunk," concluded the patrolman just before returning to his city limits. "You know how they'll wreck, then run off to hide somewhere, then report their car stolen after they sober up in the morning."

"Yeah, probably," agreed the deputy, as he began filling out his report. A tow truck arrived and hooked up to the sport utility. The officer looked over the vehicle once more, but saw no blood, no tissue; only the glasses and the cell phone. The tow truck took the wreck away, and the deputy left to visit the address to where the truck's plates were registered.

About a half-hour later, the deputy pulled up to a small apartment. A young woman answered the door. The deputy asked about the crashed sport utility.

"Yes, it's mine all right," she stated, obviously worried. "My friend John is driving it tonight. He called me on his cell phone about two ours ago and said he was coming here."

"Had he been drinking?" asked the deputy.

"Absolutely not. Not John. He doesn't drink."

"Well, like I told you, we couldn't find him anywhere around. We thought he might have tried to walk somewhere."

"I hope so," she said. "But there's one thing. Did you find his glasses?"

"There was a pair of glasses still in the truck."

The girl suddenly turned grim. "Then something must be wrong. He can't see at all without those glasses. He never goes without them."

The deputy thanked the girl and left with more questions than when he'd arrived. Where could the driver be? Remembering every detail of the scene, the deputy could not understand why the man had not been found. The search had turned up nothing. But he sensed something wasn't right, and something kept telling him to go back to where the wreck had happened.

It was even darker when he pulled to a stop on the lonely road where the crash had occurred. He looked over the skid marks again; evaluating the path the truck had taken. The ugly gash in the embankment seemed to have been made with quite a lot of force. With some apprehension, he took out his flashlight and walked out into the field.

The tall grass waved in an unseen breeze as he walked over the same ground he'd searched hours before. Still no clues. He looked back to where his patrol car sat in the road, calculating the scenario in his head. On a whim, he walked far out of the 100-foot search area, into the dark field.

He had almost given up when his light caught something in the tall grass. He walked closer, trying to make out the object that didn't seem to fit in the darkness. Then he saw the shoe.

"Dear Lord," he whispered.

The extreme forces which had made the deep gash in the roadside were now all too plain to him. There, lying in the cool grass of the field, lay the body of a young man. The victim had been thrown almost 200 feet from the crash scene, two thirds the length of a football field. It was clear he had died instantly.

An ambulance arrived and transported the body to the morgue, and the deputy amended his reports to account for the discovery of the victim. If it had not been for his intuition as a police officer, he might not have taken the extra effort to locate the man. Still, he had never seen a human body thrown so great a distance in an accident.

And he couldn't help but know the sickening truth that had the man been wearing a seatbelt, he'd have likely survived.

It's a Sad and Hopeless Place Behind Those Walls

I never saw the inside of a jail until I saw it from behind a badge. It was never a place I wanted to go; a place where the only people in my family that ever went there were those distant cousins who everybody talked bad about over Sunday dinner. Even when I was a kid, there were police officers in my family, and so anything I heard about jail was always accompanied by reference to "bad guys."

Even after I went to work as a police officer and became more familiar with jail cells, I knew it wasn't the place for me. I've seen different facilities in several counties, both in this state as well as others, and no matter how clean or nice the place was, it was still a jail. A place you can't get out of when you want to.

But something that always has surprised me is the fact that a lot of other people don't seem to mind going there. I've seen citizens cause more trouble for an officer over a traffic ticket than for being arrested. For a career criminal, it is almost as if jail is merely an occupational hazard. They try not to have to go, but if they do, it's no big deal to them. They don't seem to mind the public humiliation, the less-than-desirable food, the orange or striped uniforms, not to mention the separation from family and friends. They don't seem to mind the smell that is always present in a jail, the smell of cleaning solutions permeated with a dank, sweaty odor that seems to be on every item of clothing, every wall, and even the eating utensils. I never understood that, and I don't know if I ever will. I suppose the fact that they have free medical care, free meals, and free cable television makes it tolerable.

But I do know that for all the stress and pressure that I experienced as a patrol officer, none of it compares to the stress, working conditions, and atmosphere that corrections officers endure. It's a job that I'm not sure I could do, because, in a way, a corrections officer is just as much a prisoner as an inmate, at least for the time he is on shift. Corrections officers go to work each day to a world of depressed, angry people who have no other way of venting their frustrations than to look for ways to harass the officers or invent some way to circumvent the rules of their incarceration. This is not to say that all prisoners are bad people. In fact, there are actually some who are better people when they are locked up than when they are free. Others pay their debt to society with no incidents and never come back. But the fact remains, they are all in jail, convicted of crimes against the good of our community. And corrections officers deal with this world every day for considerably less pay than even the lowest paid patrol officer. And so, it is understandable why it is so hard to find employees willing to do such a depressing and thankless job for such a small paycheck.

Even the corrections officers at the state level have to be a "different" kind of people. Certainly, the pay is better, but the atmosphere in a large state prison is an even more "different" as well. I recall taking some prisoners on a transfer to Brushy Mountain State Penitentiary several years ago. As we got closer, the men in the back of my car became very quiet, and a strange and dreadful look come over them as we pulled up to the walls. The officers there are no-nonsense men whose stern attitudes are as large as their NFL-sized frames. When we dropped off the inmates, we were invited to take a quick tour of the prison. Some of my fellow officers accepted, but not me.

I had no desire to see the world on the other side of those walls. I did not wish to experience the lost and hopeless sensation as the giant doors close behind me, shutting off all contact with other people, with my freedom.

For me, cable TV would not be enough.

The Big, Quiet Cop

(Winston Guy was a cop in a the small town of Etowah, Tennessee, for over thirty years, and he was my grandfather. The following is one of many stories I've written about him.)

He was a big man but had a quiet nature. A textbook neighborhood cop who knew every person in the small town where he worked. His voice was always calm and soothing to any person he encountered. He treated every person he met the same, no matter what side of the law they were on. He knew that today's suspect might be tomorrow's witness, and the respect he showed his fellow citizens lives long after him.

Not a man to lose his composure, he was nonetheless tested from time to time over a thirty-plus-year career in law enforcement. The only time he fired his weapon in the line of duty was up in the air at a fleeing robbery suspect. It was a warning shot, fired to let the criminal know that he'd better stop running or the next shot would be at him. The criminal gave up and thanked the big officer for not shooting him.

Another time, he was almost not so lucky. He went to a residence in his small Tennessee town, intending to serve an arrest warrant on a suspect who lived there. It was a man he knew, and he felt no cause for concern as he knocked on the front door.

But the suspect didn't share his affection. The man pushed open the door, and shoved a loaded pistol into the officer's gut. As he pulled the trigger, the officer shoved a big hand into the pistol's hammer, preventing it from striking the bullet and firing into him. He twisted the gun from the man's hand, took him by the shirt collar and led him to the police car. The officer carried the scar on his hand for the rest of his life.

As his self-control was widely known, so was his lack of a temper. Drunks berated him, unappreciative citizens sometimes slighted him, but he carried on, rarely even taking the time to mention a strike on his integrity. But as a father and a husband, he was passionately protective.

One night, while driving his wife along the highway, the off-duty officer saw headlights approaching. It took only a horrible second for him to realize the other car was in his lane and was about to hit them head on. The big red Pontiac he was driving barely held on to the shoulder of the road as he swerved, narrowly missing the other car that flew by them. He turned around and radioed back to another on-duty officer that the reckless driver was coming into town.

By the time the other officers had the suspect stopped, the officer rolled up in his red Pontiac. He very quietly stepped up to the car where the officers stood with the driver, who turned out to be drunk and belligerent. Not realizing he was facing the man who he'd almost killed, the drunk lunged clumsily in an effort to punch the big quiet man. The other officers didn't even have time to react.

The quiet man swung one huge hand that struck the drunk directly on the side of his head, knocking him cleanly off his feet. He was unconscious before he hit the ground. The other officers lifted the man up, placing him in the squad car, respectfully watching the quiet off-duty cop that got back into the red Pontiac with his wife and drove away.

One More Servant from September

I won't ever forget the attacks of September 11, 2001. Like most Americans, I will forever recall where I was and how the images of that day affected our country and our country's future. Everyone has his or her own story about that day, and I suppose I am no different. But for me, it was not the events themselves so much as it was the response to the events that affected me the most. Because it was that day, and the days that followed, that forced me to understand my purpose as a public servant.

Nine months prior to that day, I had officially retired from public service. After I had worked over ten years in law enforcement and emergency services, my family had grown to a wife and three boys, and the meager deputy sheriff's paycheck was beginning to come up short. After much thought and prayer, I made a decision to leave public service for a much better-paying job in private industry. At the time, my responsibility to my family was paramount, and there seemed to be no other options available.

It was an extreme change for me, both in the type of work as well as the mentality and philosophy of a private business, as opposed to working for the public. I was accustomed to coming in contact with hundreds of different people each week, and every day being different. And although I enjoyed the increase in pay and found the position challenging, I missed the responsibility of being a servant of the public, knowing that thousands of people had once relied on me, that I was one of the people to call if there was a problem. What I missed the most was being able to use my training and experience to be able to respond to the needs of my community.

Then came September 11.

While the attacks were horrendous and terrible, I was moved by the lives lost by so many of the police officers, firefighters, and EMTs who were simply doing their jobs that day. I could identify with them, and I could identify with the responders who went back into the rubble and flames to do what they could. But, I was bothered by a sense of uneasiness and fear that was evident closer to home in my own community. I felt like I should be providing comfort and support and that I should be doing the things that I had always done, being there when people needed to ask a question, or needed help, or were afraid. But I was unable to do so, because I was no longer working in that capacity.

One of the hardest things I have ever done was to go back to my job that night. Never before had I felt so strongly that I should be somewhere else, that I should be doing something else. Even the money was not such a big issue anymore. In the days that followed, I realized I could not do the job in the private sector, that I would never be happy being away from the public. The talents I have been blessed with, however meager they may be, gave me a purpose that I could no longer deny. I was meant to be a servant of the public, and at my earliest opportunity, that was what I was going to go back to.

It was not so long afterward when that opportunity came, and I took it. Every day in the County Mayor's office is a blessing and an opportunity to use skills and experience working with a multitude of people as well as industries, federal, state, and other local government officials. It's an office where public service is not just a slogan; it is practiced every day with a philosophy of "leadership through service." Whether assisting a department-head in obtaining grant funds, providing assistance to an organization's board of directors, or simply helping a citizen find a resource he is in need of, I know I am where I am supposed to be. September 11 helped me to realize who I was and what I should be doing; how important service is to my community and my country.

That fateful day, terrorists intended to bring down buildings and instill fear in America. They succeeded in bringing together a country and strengthening our resolve and our patriotism. They probably never realized they would be so unsuccessful in what they were actually trying to accomplish.

And they probably never realized they'd return one more servant to the cause of his community and his country.

How the Lord Made Cops

Police officers' hearts can often be hardened by the bad things they see every day. Even so, many find strength and consolation in prayer and spirituality to help them deal with stress and anxiety. About a year ago, someone sent me the following anonymous story off of the Internet that tells a fictional account of how the Lord made cops. It struck a cord with me, as well as with other officers, judges, and attorneys who read it.

How the Lord Created Police Officers

When the Lord started creating police officers, he was into his sixth day of overtime when an angel happened by and noticed, "You are doing a lot of fiddling around on this one."

The Lord replied, "Have you seen the 'spec' on this order? A police officer has to be able to run five miles through alleys in the dark, scale walls, enter homes the health inspector wouldn't touch and not wrinkle his uniform.

"He has to be able to sit in an undercover car all day on a stakeout, cover a homicide scene that night, canvass the neighborhood for witnesses and testify in court early the next morning.

"He has to be in top physical condition at all times, running on black coffee and half-eaten meals, and he has to have six pairs of hands," the Lord added.

The angel shook his head slowly and said, "Six pairs of hands...No way."

But the Lord explained, "It is not the hands that are causing me the problem. It is the three pairs of eyes an officer has to have."

"That's on the standard model?" asked the angel.

The Lord nodded. "One pair that sees through the bulge in a pocket before he asks, 'May I see what's in there, sir?' (When he already knows and wishes he'd taken an accounting job).

"Another pair here on the side of his head to watch after his partner's safety. And another pair of eyes here in front that can look reassuringly at a bleeding victim and say, 'You'll be alright, Ma'am,' when he knows that it isn't so."

"Lord," said the angel, touching his sleeve, "rest and work on this tomorrow."

"I can't," replied the Lord, "I already have a model that can talk a 250-pound drunk into the back of a patrol car and feed a family of five on a civil service paycheck."

The angel circled the model of the police officer very slowly. "Can it think?" he asked.

"You bet," came the reply. "It can tell you the elements of hundreds of crimes and recite the Miranda warning in its sleep, detain, investigate, search, and arrest a gang member on the street in less time it takes five learned judges to debate the legality of the stop...and it still keeps its sense of humor."

"The officer also has phenomenal personal control. He can deal with crime scenes painted in hell, coax a confession out of a child abuser, comfort a murder victim's family, and then read in the daily newspaper a long story under the headline 'Law Enforcement Isn't Sensitive to the Rights of Criminal Suspects.'"

Finally the angel bent over and ran his finger across the cheek of the police officer. "There's a leak," he pronounced. "I told you that you were trying too much on this model."

"That's not a leak," the Lord said, "that's a tear."

"What's the tear for?"

"It's for bottled up emotions, for fallen comrades, for commitment to that funny piece of cloth called the American flag, for justice."

"You're a genius," the angel said. But the Lord remained somber.

"I didn't put it there."

You Stuck It Where?

The mental health specialist drove up to the country jail, parking her car in the moonlit parking lot. She gathered her paperwork together and stepped inside. The desk clerk recognized her immediately.

"You look sleepy," said the clerk.

"It's 3:00AM. What do you expect? Is she still awake?"

The clerk nodded. "Oh, yeah she's still awake. She's lucky, this one. If the officer hadn't been there, it could have been bad. Come on, I'll take you back."

The mental health specialist followed the clerk to an interview room where, at the table, sat a thin, middle-aged woman with short blonde hair. She was taking a drag on her cigarette and barely seemed to notice the mental health worker who introduced herself and sat down.

"I'm just here to talk to you," said the professional. "They tell me you tried to hurt yourself tonight."

The woman nodded, blew out a mist of smoke. "I just been, you know, depressed and stuff. I don't know why I did it."

"That's why I'm here. Tell me about what happened, and maybe I can find you some treatment to help you feel better."

Between draws on her cigarette, the thin blonde woman told her story. Depression, drug use, and an abusive relationship, the mental health specialist had heard it all before. She took careful notes, and when the interview was completed, she made a few calls and found a program that might make a difference, though probably not.

During the interview, the thin woman revealed that her method of suicide had been to take an overdose of pills, but as she was taking them, a deputy arrived at her home, called by a concerned relative. Somehow, the deputy had kept the woman from completing her plan. Curious, the mental health specialist went back to the interview room and asked the woman an off-handed question.

"What happened with the deputy? What kept you from taking all the pills?"

The woman puffed her cigarette. "I was trying to take them all, but he came in just as I started. I slammed the door, but he broke in and stopped me."

"Hmmm. I see," said the specialist as she read over the arrest report. "It also says you were charged with bringing a controlled substance into the jail. How did you do that?"

"Before the deputy broke in, I hid my pill bottle on me."

"Where did you hide the pill bottle?"

"In my vagina," replied the thin woman. She took another drag off her cigarette.

The mental health specialist was taken aback by what the woman was implying against the officer. She had to know more.

"So if you'd hidden the bottle of pills in your vagina, how in the world did the deputy find them?"

The thin woman showed no emotion. She crushed out her cigarette, blew out a long stream of smoke, and said,

"When I was walking up to the booking desk, he heard 'em."

About the Author

Joe D. Guy is a nationally published author, syndicated newspaper columnist, historian, storyteller, and lecturer from McMinn County in East Tennessee. His articles on school safety and officer-community relations have appeared in *Community Policing Exchange* and *Community Links*, and were widely recognized by school systems and law enforcement agencies across the country. Mr. Guy's popular syndicated newspaper column, "Beyond the Blue Line," is drawn from stories he has collected during his career as a police officer, deputy sheriff, EMT, SWAT team commander, and detective. Writers Club Press published a collection of the articles, Beyond the Blue Line: Stories From the Other Side of Law Enforcement, in 2002.

A student of history, Mr. Guy is also the author of the historical narrative Indian Summer: The Siege and Fall of Fort Loudoun (The Overmountain Press, 2001), which has received excellent reviews among newspapers, historical groups, and tourism associations. He also writes a weekly syndicated column, "Hidden History," which is based on the regional history of Southeast Tennessee. Other historical articles have appeared in *Appalachian Life Magazine*, *Backwoodsman Magazine*, and in *McMinn County: A History of Its People.* Mr. Guy was a 2000 and 2002 scholarship winner in both fiction and non-fiction to the Lost State Writers Conference.

Currently, Mr. Guy is the Special Projects Director and Assistant to the County Mayor in McMinn County, Tennessee, where he resides with his wife and children. He is also the McMinn County Historian.

What People Are Saying About Joe Guy

A Sample of Reviews:

Beyond the Blue Line, Volume 1

"...a very entertaining book...a different perspective..." *Barnes and Noble.com*

"...an extremely popular column...gives an unique view on the world of a police officer...look forward to his stories every week..." *Daily Post-Athenian*

Indian Summer

"...no other work has included such a comprehensive and intriguing story related to the Fort Loudoun saga..." *Tennessee Overhill Heritage Association*

"...succinctly tells the story of Fort Loudoun...a fuller impact of its history..."
Knoxville News-Sentinel

Printed in the United States
69423LVS00002B/177

9 781413 782028